THE GREAT BRITISH
SEWING BEE
THE MODERN
WARDROBE

THE GREAT BRITISH SEWING BEE
THE MODERN WARDROBE

JULIET UZOR

FOREWORDS BY
PATRICK GRANT & ESME YOUNG

PHOTOGRAPHY BY
**BROOKE HARWOOD &
CHARLOTTE MEDLICOTT**

Hardie Grant

QUADRILLE

Contents

FOREWORD BY

Patrick Grant

I never actually set out to have a career in fashion,
but it's been a major part of my life for more years
than I care to remember. Never in my wildest dreams,
however, would I have imagined that making clothes
would be the subject of a prime-time television series
– let alone that I'd end up judging *The Great British
Sewing Bee* for (at the time of writing) eight whole
series! But I love seeing how every contestant brings
their personal style to the challenges we set them.
Even though they all start from the same base pattern,
it never ceases to amaze me that the garments look so
different. Yes, of course the technical side is important
– I certainly don't want to see raw edges or gaping
holes in seams or garments that sag or pinch in all
the wrong places. But when individuality and creativity
combine with technical prowess, then you've got
something really special.

Maybe that's one of the reasons why *The Great British
Sewing Bee* is so popular – those magical moments
when, despite all the drama and angst, everything
comes together and you end up with not just a flawless
piece of sewing but with colour or fabric combinations
that make your heart sing. It's certainly what gives me
the biggest buzz. Every single series, I see something
completely new and innovative that inspires me in
my own work. I hope this latest *Sewing Bee* book will
encourage you to try out new styles and techniques
for yourself and, whether you're a relative newcomer
or someone who's been making clothes for years,
help you on your sewing journey.

FOREWORD BY

Esme Young

Sewing is such a meditative process – you have to slow down and focus, blocking out any other distractions, and that's got to be good for your health and wellbeing. What's more, you're always learning something. I've been sewing since I was seven, when I was taught to sew at school, but I'm still learning – and in my eyes the biggest mistake any sewist can make is to think they know it all, because no one ever can.

I can still remember the first thing I made – a red gathered skirt that I must have sewn by hand, because we didn't have sewing machines. It probably wasn't anything special, but I was so proud of it! That joy has never left me. Sewing is creative – you start out with a flat piece of fabric that you turn into something three-dimensional and you really feel as if you've achieved something.

Since that first red skirt, I've gone on to study graphics at Central Saint Martin's in London, worked as a fashion designer and costume maker in films, and now I've come full circle. I'm back at Central Saint Martin's teaching pattern cutting and all of these widely differing experiences feed into my judging on *The Great British Sewing Bee.* So what do I look for as a judge? Well, I look for attention to detail: beautiful seams, even hems, good pattern matching, carefully chosen trims, no puckering. And as regular viewers will know, I do love a big bow! I want everything to be perfect, but I also want to be surprised; above all, I want to see the contestants' personalities show through in their choice of fabric, their choice of colours, the sewing techniques they use. I've always encouraged the *Great British Sewing Bee* contestants to make something from scratch to their own taste and style rather than using a shop-bought pattern – and I urge you to do the same. So use the patterns in this book as a starting point, then mix and match different elements to come up with something that's truly yours. Once you've taken the plunge and started deviating from the 'official' pattern, I promise you you'll find it thoroughly liberating and your creativity will flourish!

Introduction

This latest *Great British Sewing Bee* book – sub-titled 'The Modern Wardrobe' – features patterns for a core wardrobe of garments, from a simple A-line skirt and casual trousers to more tailored dresses and blouses. There are some garments that you may recognize from the TV show, while others have been created especially for this book, but all the designs lend themselves to the creation of different items of clothing – so once you've tried out the base patterns, you can alter them to add personal touches and customize the designs.

I've grouped together garments that are similar in construction or technique to give you some idea of the range of options available to you. I've included patterns for all the garments in the book, so you can follow them to the letter if you want to – but for those of you who'd like to branch out a little, I've also dropped in some ideas on how you can ring the changes and make something truly your own. Some alterations are obvious – for example, you could lengthen a basic top to create a simple shift dress or add a patch pocket to a skirt front. You'll also see how making the same pattern in a different weight of fabric can completely change the look, as in the Faux Pleat Dress and Top (pages 148 and 156). Other variations are based around a particular technique to show you how many different looks you can create once you've mastered the basic method. You'll see this in the shirred garments on pages 86–107, where the shirring technique that's

often associated with informal 'country-style' dresses is also used to make a sophisticated blouse for evening wear. You can also mix and match between patterns, perhaps removing the darts from a simple pair of trousers and attaching them to a wrap-over top to form a jumpsuit, or removing the bodice section of a dress and changing the waistband to create a stylish skirt for work, as in the Wrap Dress and Wrap Skirt (pages 70 and 76).

Other adaptions require a little more planning – and for these it's a good idea to sew a toile (see page 24). You can give a loose-fitting top more shape by adding bust darts or remove darts for a more relaxed look. You can change the shape of a neckline, as I did when I adapted the Classic Breton Top pattern (page 162) to make a Cropped Top with a more boxy neckline and shorter sleeves (page 168). You could add sleeves to a sleeveless top to create a statement piece, as in the Long-sleeved Shell Top on page 218, or even slash through a bodice to add a style line.

I hope this approach will allow you to use the patterns to their full potential – and that's surely the aim of all home sewers looking to create beautiful pieces for their wardrobes without breaking the bank. Use this book for inspiration to create clothes that you love – the options are endless!

How to Use this Book

PATTERNS TO ACCOMPANY THE BOOK

This book comes with full-scale patterns nested in multiple sizes, which can be downloaded as a PDF at https://www.hardiegrant.com/uk/quadrille/themodernwardrobe for you to print at home or at a copy shop.

Once printed and pieced together, trace the pattern pieces onto dressmaker's carbon paper, making sure you follow the lines for your size, then cut out. You will find information on adjusting patterns to fit your body shape and 'grading' patterns between sizes on pages 12–19.

The outside lines on the pattern pieces are the cutting lines. Different sizes have different line types such as solid, dotted or dashed, which are also numbered by size. In some areas the lines merge, so it is advisable to go over your size line with a coloured pencil before tracing.

UK women's sizing

————————————	8
· · · · · · · · · · · · · · · · ·	10
— — — — — — — —	12
—··—··—··—··—·	14
——————————	16
—— ——— ——— ——— ——— ——— ——	18
—— ——— — —— ——	20
————————————	22

TOP TIP

In the step-by-step illustrations accompanying the projects, the right of the fabric is shown as a dark tone and the wrong side as a light tone.

LAY PLANS

The lay plans included in this book indicate how each project should be cut out – where the grain line on the pattern should be placed, whether pieces should be cut on the fold or not. Check each lay plan when pinning your pattern pieces to your fabric.

The majority of the projects in this book are to be cut with the fabric folded in half right side to right side, with the selvedges together, so that you get perfectly symmetrical pieces when cutting on the fold and perfectly matching pairs when cutting two pieces that need to be identical (such as sleeves). If just a single pattern piece is to be cut, rather than a pair, that piece is coloured grey on the lay plans. Occasionally you are required to cut the fabric flat, and not on the fold. This is the case when a pattern piece is wider than the folded fabric. These lay plans are labelled 'single layer'.

DIFFICULTY LEVELS

Each project in this book is given a difficulty level – beginners, intermediate or confident sewer.

Sewing Pattern Adjustments

Checking for fit and making pattern adjustments

One of the main reasons to make your own clothes is to get garments to fit properly instead of trying to fit into standardized sizes, so the first step is to choose the correct pattern size. To do that you need to take accurate measurements. Never assume you are the same size pattern as you are ready-to-wear.

MEASURING

To achieve the best results when measuring it is important to measure over the undergarments you normally wear, as that is what you will be wearing underneath. Don't measure over clothes. The bust, waist and hip measurements are used to determine your pattern size – but you may very well be a different size pattern for bust, waist and indeed hip. This is quite normal, very few people are the perfect pattern size. But with multi-sized patterns you can quite easily cut from one size cutting line to another and back again. Mixing up pattern pieces also allows you to 'hack' the designs and create your own unique version of the garment – see Customizing and Adapting Patterns on page 20 for more information. Think of the patterns provided as 'templates', onto which you can build your designs.

Bust

Measure around the fullest part of the bust, usually at nipple height, and straight across the back. The high bust measurement is taken directly under the arms, straight across the back and above the bust.

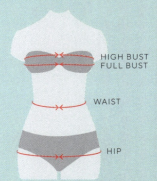

HIGH BUST
FULL BUST

WAIST

HIP

Waist

If not obvious (and as we get older, it often isn't!), tie a narrow elastic or string around your middle and bend slightly from side to side to allow it to settle naturally at your waistline. Measure over the elastic. Keep the elastic in place for the next measurement.

Hip

The hip is the widest part of your bottom and upper thighs. Measure with your feet together around the body, usually 18 to 23 cm (7 to 9 in.) below the waist. The measurement around your hip bones is called the high hip.

These are the main measurements you will need to take to determine pattern size, but when adjusting patterns you might also find the following useful:

....

TOP TIP

Hold the tape measure comfortably snug but not tight. You might find it helpful to enlist a friend to do the measuring, as it's easier to take measurements on someone else.

....

Back waist length

From the most prominent bone at the nape/base of neck to the natural waistline.

Height

Measure your height barefoot against a wall.

CHOOSING YOUR SIZE

Dresses, tops, jackets

If you have more than 6.5 cm (2½ in.) difference between bust and high bust, select your pattern size by HIGH BUST measurement). You will then need to alter the pattern to fit the fuller bust, but it should fit better across shoulders, chest and torso. For pattern alteration tips, see pages 14–19.

Skirts and trousers

Use your waist measurement unless your hips are two sizes or more larger than your waist, then use your hip measurement.

Between two sizes

For a closer fit or if you are small boned, select the smaller size. For a looser fit or if you are big boned, select the larger size.

Most female patterns are designed for a woman who is 1.65 m to 1.67 m (5 ft 5 in. to 5 ft 6 in.). If you are taller or shorter, you may have to adjust the pattern length (see page 15).

Standard ready-to-wear measurements

UK size	8	10	12	14	16	18	20	22
Bust (cm)	83	88	93	98	103	108	113	118
Bust (in.)	32½	34½	36½	38½	40½	42½	44½	46½
Waist (cm)	64	69	74	79	84	89	94	99
Waist (in.)	25	27	29	31	33	35	37	39
Hip (cm)	90	95	100	105	110	115	120	125
Hip (in.)	35½	37½	39½	41½	43¼	45¼	47¼	49¼

MAKING PATTERN ADJUSTMENTS

Having established your measurements you can then adjust the pattern at the points necessary so that the final garment will fit perfectly. With commercial patterns, most of the adjustments you'll be making will be lengthening and shortening. However, it's also useful to be able to move darts and to make bust adjustments if necessary.

GRADING PATTERNS BETWEEN SIZES

The beauty of having all pattern sizes on the same pattern sheet is that you can easily grade in between the different sizes to suit your measurements. Use dressmakers' tracing paper, which is see through and is available in packs containing large sheets suitable for big pattern pieces. Other paper, such as dot-and-cross or baking parchment paper, can be used but may have to be pieced together first.

Spread out the pattern sheet that includes the pieces you need. Lay the tracing paper on top, smoothed flat and anchored in place with weights. Blend one size into another as you trace off the design. If you are a size 16 on the bust and waist but a size 18 on the hips, for example, you can draw in a smooth line from 16 to 18 in between the waist and the hip to achieve a more

personal pattern. You can use a pattern master or a French curve for this to get a really smooth line. It's a great idea to do this in a colour so you can see where to cut when you have finished grading.

Another way to easily add a bit more space into a pattern is to add to the centre back if you have a seam there. The centre back seam is a straight line, so this way you can easily add up to 2.5 cm (1 in.) without having to redraw side seams, which will typically have some shaping to them.

....

TOP TIP

If a commercial pattern has each size on separate sheets, you can layer the relevant sheets up first as the tissue the pieces are printed on are thin enough to see through. Then lay your tracing paper over the top and grade as shown below left.

....

ALTERING THE LENGTH

Sometimes you need more or less length in a pattern – for example, because your upper body is tall/short or because you have long/short legs. You can determine whether you need more or less length in a bodice by taking your nape-to-waist measurement and comparing that to the pattern. If lengthening or shortening is necessary, this is the first alteration you should make.

Some patterns have a line that indicates where you can shorten and lengthen, which is positioned in such a way that it doesn't interfere with things like darts. If you don't see a line on your pattern, you can always add or remove length at the bottom of a pattern if it's a question of a longer or shorter hem, or draw a horizontal line across the pattern. If you are lengthening or shortening by more than 2.5 cm (1 in.), you may want to do it in two different places so as not to disturb the design of the pattern too much.

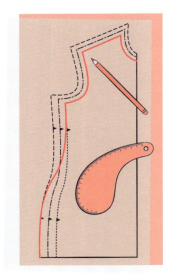

LENGTHENING

Cut your pattern across the lengthen/shorten line and spread the pattern pieces apart by the amount that you need. If you are adding length in two different places and you want to add 5 cm (2 in.) in total, spread by 2.5 cm (1 in.) in each area. Slide a piece of paper behind and stick your new pattern down with tape. Make sure to line up all vertical lines on the pattern, such as the grain line. Then use a ruler or a French curve to smooth out the outlines of your new pattern. This is called trueing.

SHORTENING

Fold the pattern across the lengthen/shorten line or draw a horizontal line across the pattern. Then make a tuck that's half the amount you want to shorten by: if you want to shorten by 3 cm (1¼ in.), for example, make a 1.5-cm (⅝-in.) tuck. Use tape to stick down the tucks and redraw any outside lines that need smoothing out.

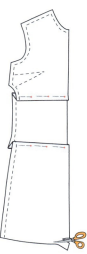

TOP TIP

The seam allowance is the distance between the stitching and the fabric edge. The amount needed depends on the project, but generally for dressmaking it is 1.5 cm (⅝ in.). It is very important that you are consistent and use the correct seam allowance noted in the pattern instructions when stitching, or the garment will not fit properly despite any adjustments you have made.

ADJUSTING THE BACK

If you find that clothes strain at the back, and you end up buying a bigger size that then doesn't fit your front, then the chances are you have a broad back. If clothes stand away from your spine along the centre of your back, then a narrow back adjustment can help. This is the real beauty of dressmaking: we can fine-tune the fit exactly where we need it.

Narrow back

1   Some patterns come with an adjustment line for narrow or broad backs drawn on. If your pattern doesn't, draw a vertical line down from the shoulder, starting 3 cm (1¼ in.) from the armhole and ending just below the bottom of the armhole. Draw a second line out to the side of the pattern at a right angle from the bottom of the first line.

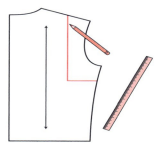

2   Cut along the two lines to separate the armhole piece and slide it over towards the centre back, overlapping the paper. Generally around 6 mm (¼ in.) is enough but you can play around with this distance to suit your own needs. Stick the pattern paper in place. Use a ruler and pencil to redraw the side seam into a smooth line.

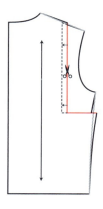

3 Check the resulting shoulder length and adjust the shoulder length on the front pattern piece accordingly. Note if you take in more than just 6mm (¼ in.) you may have to adjust the sleeve head of a sleeve.

Broad back

1 Draw the lines as in step 1 for a narrow back, and cut out the armhole section.

2 Instead of overlapping the pattern pieces, spread them apart. Again there are no set rules, but a 6 to 13 mm (¼ to ½ in.) adjustment is usually sufficient. Fill in the space created with some pattern paper and stick the pieces together. Use a ruler and pencil to match up and redraw the outside of the side seam.

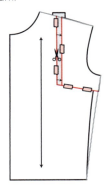

3 Again you will need to adjust the shoulder length of the front pattern piece, making it a little longer to match the back.

Waist dart manipulation

An easy way to adapt patterns that have waist darts is to take in the darts a bit more or less than the pattern requires. This is suitable for small pattern alterations to the waist. Divide the alteration between the number of darts – so if you want to take in the waist by 2 cm (¾ in.) and you have four darts, make each dart 5 mm (³⁄₁₆ in.) more than the pattern. The same goes for adding space to the waist: reduce the darts slightly to make the waist a bit bigger.

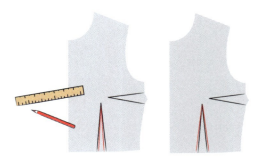

BUST ADJUSTMENTS

You may need to alter the fit at the bust in three ways: to accommodate for a small or full bust, or to move the bust point on the bust dart. The bust point is the fullest point of your bust, which can sit higher or lower on each woman. Measure your own bust point from the shoulder down and compare it to the pattern.

Moving a bust dart up or down

Your bust may not be at the same height as the one on the pattern, so you may need to raise or lower the bust darts. Darts are angled, making them a little awkward to re-draw freehand. This technique is simple and there is no complicated geometry involved, plus all the shaping at the side seam remains intact.

1 With a ruler, draw a rectangular box around the bust dart. Cut around the box and move it up or down, keeping the edges of the rectangle parallel to the original position.

2 Tape the box to its new position and slide a piece of paper behind the pattern to fill the gap. Use a ruler and perhaps a French curve to match up and redraw the outline of your new pattern.

Full or small bust adjustment

Most commercial patterns are cut to fit a B cup, which means some of us will have to adapt our patterns to fit our bust measurements. This can seem more daunting than it is but it will make a big difference to how your clothes fit. The advantage of sewing a garment from scratch is that you can make these adjustments early on and create a garment that will fit much better than a shop-bought item.

If your full bust measurement is bigger than your high bust measurement by more than 6.5 cm (2½ in.), you will need to do a full bust adjustment (FBA). If this is the case, use your high bust measurement as your bust size to determine which pattern size to cut from the size chart. If the difference between your high and full bust is much smaller than 6.5 cm (2½ in.), you may need a small bust adjustment (SBA).

The process for doing a full or small bust adjustment is the same, except that you are either adding space by spreading the pattern or reducing space by overlapping the pattern.

Think about the kind of garment you are making before you adjust your pattern. These adjustments are great for garments with fitted bodices, but are not strictly necessary for floaty garments with lots of ease.

Full bust adjustment (FBA)

1 Lay the tissue pattern against yourself to establish where your bust point or apex is. Mark this on the pattern with a cross. Using a ruler and pencil, draw a vertical line from the marked point to the hem. Make sure that this line is parallel to the grain line on the pattern. From the top of this vertical line, draw another line up towards the armhole, hitting the lower third of the armhole. Together these two lines are called Line 1. Draw a second line horizontally through the middle of the bust dart, meeting Line 1 at the bust point.

2 Cut along Line 1 from the hem to the armhole, making sure you do not cut all the way through the armhole. Leave a hinge so that you can pivot the paper. The point of the dart has now swung away from its original position. Cut through the line in the middle of the dart, again leaving a little hinge at the tip of the dart so you can pivot.

3 Line up the cut edges of Line 1 so they've been spread apart by the amount of your FBA. The vertical edges should be parallel to one another. You'll notice that your dart has now spread apart, too, and become bigger. The lower edge of your hem no longer meets at the bottom, as the side that has been adjusted is now longer. Draw a third line parallel to the bottom edge, cut along it and spread the pieces apart until your hem is level. Fill in the spaces created with tracing paper, and stick into place.

Small bust adjustment (SBA)

1 Draw in the lines as per an FBA adjustment. This is essentially the same process as an FBA adjustment in reverse. Draw in the lines on the pattern, and cut along them in exactly the same way as for an FBA adjustment.

2 Pivot the darted side of the pattern across the other side by the desired SBA amount.

3 The lower edge of the hem no longer meets at the bottom, as the side that has been adjusted is now shorter. Cut along the third line you drew, and overlap the pattern pieces until your hem is level.

ADJUSTING BODICE PATTERNS WITHOUT DARTS

If your pattern does not have a bust dart, you can make the FBA by creating your own dart. Measure up from the waist 15 cm (6 in.) along the side edge and mark with a dot. Draw a straight line from this mark to the bust point on the pattern. Again draw a straight line from the lower third of the armhole to the bust point and then from there down to the lower edge, as before. Slash and spread the pattern paper by the required amount, add extra pattern paper and tape in place. Now to close up the side opening created, draw a dart equal to the width of the side opening with the tip of the dart 2.5 cm (1 in.) from the bust point. Lengthen the centre front as noted above.

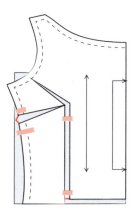

TROUSER ADJUSTMENTS

There are two common adjustments you can easily make to trouser patterns: the crotch depth and the crotch length. The crotch depth is the distance between your waist and the crotch line on the pattern and is what defines the rise of your trousers. It can vary enormously between person to person, depending on body shape. The crotch length is the measurement taken from the front of the waist, between your legs to the back waist.

Adjusting the crotch depth

To measure this, sit on a hard chair and measure the distance from your waist to the seat. Check your measurement against the waist to crotch line on the pattern (remember to measure from the seam line at the waist).

The process of adjusting the crotch depth is basically the same as lengthening and shortening a dress or skirt (see page 15). Draw a horizontal line across the trouser pattern along the hip line and add the required amount of extra paper to lengthen, or fold a tuck if you need to shorten.

Adjusting the crotch length

1 Measure yourself and then compare your measurement to the curved crotch seam on the pattern – if different, divide the difference by half. This gives you the measurement you will need to spread or reduce the curve by.

2 With both front and back trouser pieces on a flat surface, mark a point 8 cm (3 in.) below the waistline on both crotch seams. Draw a horizontal line from this mark to the side seam on both pieces. Cut along the lines, leaving a hinge at the side seams.

3 To increase the crotch length, spread the pattern apart by the amount calculated in step 1, hinging at the side seams. Fill in the gap with pattern paper and tape in place.

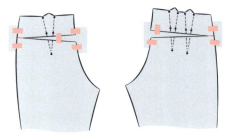

4 To reduce the crotch length, overlap the pattern pieces at the crotch by by the amount calculated in step 1 and tape in place.

Customizing and adapting patterns

Another great reason to make your own clothes is that you can make them completely individual. Many people will use the same pattern, but each one will choose different fabrics, buttons, trims, so each garment will look slightly different. If you want to take this a step further, you can customize the pattern to your exact needs, or change some of the design features to make it look completely different – a variation to the original design that is often called a hack. Here are a few ideas.

SLASH AND SPREAD TECHNIQUE

A great method to hack a pattern is to use a technique called slash and spread. With this easy method you can turn a fitted shape into a flared shape: a straight sleeve can become a bell sleeve, an A-line skirt can turn into a more flared skirt, a straight trouser leg can turn into a flared leg. It is demonstrated here on a sleeve pattern, but once you give it a go you can experiment!

1   Draw vertical lines down your sleeve pattern and cut along these lines, leaving a hinge at the sleeve head. If you draw all the way up to the sleeve head you will get a sleeve that is flared all the way from the top of the sleeve. If you would like a bishop sleeve, you can draw a horizontal line first where you want the volume to start, and then draw vertical lines up to meet this line.

2   You can now spread the different sections by equal amounts, but leaving the sleeve head the same. This means nothing changes in your armhole.

3   Slide pattern paper behind your new pattern and stick your pattern down with tape. Make sure to smooth out the hem.

The variations to this are pretty much endless. You can reverse this hack by slashing and spreading into the sleeve head to create a gathered sleeve head, or gather your new sleeve into a cuff.

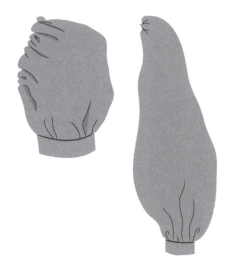

UPCYCLING THE LOOK

Simple changes can alter the look of a garment – and slightly more complex ones can make it look completely different. Just using an alternative fabric can make a casual garment into something more formal – see Changing the Fabric on page 30. Embroidery is a creative way of giving an item of clothing a fresh new look – you can find instructions online for most of the basic stitches. It can also be used to fix clothes that have small stains or damaged areas, as can appliqué. You can also use a trim to bring focus to a design detail of a garment, such as lace along a yoke seam, or ribbon highlighting a shaped hem. If a pattern is for something quite loose and wide, consider making it more fitted with shirring (see page 93), gathers (see page 39) or darts (see page 42). The simple hems on a pair of trousers could become turn-ups instead (see page 65). It's also possible to combine pattern pieces from different patterns – for instance, a loose sleeve could be made more tailored with a fitted cuff, or you could change the collar style by using the pattern pieces and instructions from a different pattern.

SEAM-INSERTED PIPING

Piping can be inserted into a seam around the edge to give a crisp finish, or as a contrast decorative detail between two pieces.

1 The piping needs to be stitched right side up onto the right side of the fabric piece along the stitching line. You may find the seam allowance on the piping is narrower than the seam allowance on the garment, in which case, match the stitching line of the piping with the stitching line of the fabric, making sure both stitching lines are perfectly aligned along the entire length of the piping. Tack (baste) just inside the stitching line, checking the alignment as you go. Use a zip foot to stitch it into position.

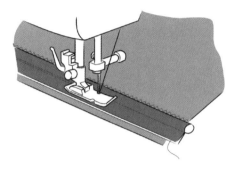

2 Lay the piece with the piping stitched to it right side up on a flat surface. Lay the piece to be stitched to it right sides down on top. Match the raw edges, pin the seam and then stitch.

3 The seam will now consist of up to four layers. If it is bulky, use a sharp pair of scissors to cut the top layer close to the stitching, the second layer a little longer, and so on, so that the layers are tapered.

FRILLS

Adding a frill at the hem can not only be a decoration but can extend the length of a dress or act as a peplum on a blouse. For more information on sewing frills, see the Ra-Ra Skirt (page 121) and the Midi Dance Skirt (page 118).

ADDING PATCH POCKETS

Adding a patch pocket is a simple alteration that you can make on both a garment as you construct it, or on a ready-made item. It doesn't matter if you don't have the same fabric as the background as contrast patch pockets can be quite a feature.

1 Use a patch pocket pattern piece from another pattern, or just draw up a suitable size rectangle with rounded bottom edges for your pocket pattern. You can also shape your pocket with a V or curved bottom edge. Cut out one piece for each pocket. Apply a 2-cm (¾-in.) wide strip of interfacing along the top edges of the pocket.

2 Along the top edge of the pockets, press 1.5 cm (⅝ in.) to the wrong side, then press under the interfaced 2 cm (¾ in.) to create a strong top edge. Topstitch in place.

3 Press 1.5 cm (⅝ in.) to the wrong side of the pocket all around the curved edges. Fold the top corners of the seam allowance in diagonally, so they won't peep out of the pocket.

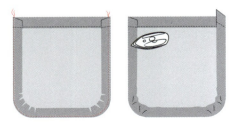

4 Place the pockets on the right side of the garment and move them around until you are happy with the positioning. Pin in place, using plenty of pins to control the curves. Lower your stitch length to about 2.5 to create a smooth stitch line, and topstitch all around the U-shape.

ADDING POCKET FLAPS

1 Use a pocket flap pattern piece from another pattern, or draw up a suitable size rectangle for your pocket pattern. The flaps shown here have a V-shape bottom edge and a buttonhole, but you could just make a plain rectangular flap. Cut out two pieces for each flap.

2 Pin two pocket flap pieces right sides together, then sew along the short sides and the bottom edge. Trim the seam allowance and clip into the corners. Turn right side out and use a bamboo pointer to get neat corners. Press well. Overlock (serge) the remaining open edges together. You can topstitch along the edges of the pocket flap for a neat effect. Make a vertical buttonhole close to the point of the V-shape. Repeat with the remaining pocket flap pieces.

3 Place the pocket flap upside down above the pocket, with the overlocked edge about 1 cm (⅜ in.) away from the pocket's top edge. Sew  along the overlocked edge with a regular seam allowance, then press the flap down into its correct position and topstitch 6 mm (¼ in.) away from the top edge to hold the flap down. Mark where the buttonhole hits the pocket and attach a button.

EXPOSED ZIP

Zips can be mounted in full, glorious view as a design detail. This method just has the teeth on view, with no stitching visible on the right side of the garment.

1 Neaten the raw edges of the seam allowances into which the zip is to be inserted. Press. Fuse 2.5-cm (1-in.) strips of interfacing to the wrong side of the zip placement area on each piece.

2 On the wrong side of the fabric, mark the zip placement lines, marking the length to just below the zip stop and the sides 2 cm (¾ in.) either side of the neatened edges. Hand or machine tack (baste) along the marked lines.

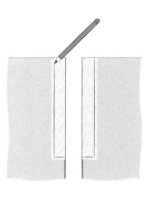

3 Snip diagonally into the seam allowances, starting 1 cm (⅜ in.) above the end of the tacking and down towards the corners, making sure you don't clip the basting stitching.

4 Fold the seam allowance of the zip placement areas to the wrong side along the tacking stitches and press.

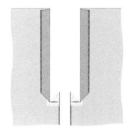

5 With right sides together, stitch the remaining seam from the horizontal tacking line down to the hem, taking a 1.5-cm seam (⅝-in.) allowance. (Note this will NOT line up with the folded zip placement area, which has been folded at 2 cm/¾ in.).

6 Press the seam allowances open. Note that, above the seam, the zip opening has a gap and the little triangles of fabric are pointing up.

7 Flip the garment so that the right side is uppermost and pin the zip right side down, with the zip stop end just below the horizontal tacking and the zip pull towards the hem. Stitch across the bottom of the zip, in line with the previous tacking – just across the centre of the zip, not all the way across the zip tape.

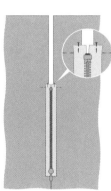

8 Flip the zip up and push it to the inside of the garment, so that only the teeth are exposed from the right side. On the wrong side, the little triangles of fabric should now be pointing downwards.

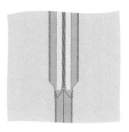

9 Turn the garment right side out and anchor the zip tape to the seam allowance only, by tacking (basting) using clips. Turn back one side so that only the seam allowance is uppermost, with the zip tape in place underneath. Machine sew down the vertical tacking stitches. Repeat for the other side of the zip.

10 Turn the garment over and you will see a beautifully inserted zip with the teeth exposed.

MANDARIN COLLAR TO PUSSYCAT BOW

A pattern with a mandarin collar can be adjusted so the collar extends into a tie at the front for a softer look.

1 Cut the two pieces for the mandarin collar following the original pattern – this will be the back neck tie piece. For the front neck ties, cut two long pieces on the fold, tapering them gently out in width from the width of the collar to a wider point at the end.

2 With right sides together, pin one front necktie piece to each side of the back necktie piece. Sew the seams and press the seam allowances open. With right sides together, fold the entire tie in half lengthwise and sew the front sections of the tie up to the point where the fronts join the back. Trim the seam allowances of the front sections and turn the tie right side out. Try to get nice sharp corners on the fronts of the tie and press the front sections.

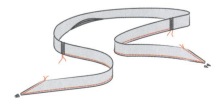

3 Press one edge of the back section of the tie under by 1.5 cm (⅝ in.). With right sides together, pin the unpressed edge of the tie to the neckline of the blouse, matching the front of the neckline to the seam in the tie and matching the notch to the shoulder seam. The necktie will be lying upside down on top of the outside of the blouse. Sew, then press the necktie and all seam allowances upwards. Then align the remaining side of the necktie (the one you pressed earlier) to the inside of the neckline and sew from the outside by stitching 'in the ditch' (see page 40). Alternatively, slipstitch the necktie in place from the inside.

Making a toile

If you're using a new pattern or are unfamiliar with a technique, it's worth making a toile – a mock-up in a plain fabric such as calico (muslin) that you can make adjustments to before cutting out your garment fabric. You could keep old sheets for this – but if the fabric you're using for the actual garment has a very different feel or drape, it's better to find an inexpensive version for your toile. Toiles are useful for close-fitting garments in a non-stretchy fabric or ones with bodice darts or seam lines hat need to be in just the right place. Anything loose fitting is easier to adjust as you sew.

1   Press and straighten the fabric so the grain is straight. Pin the pattern pieces on, aligning the grain of the fabric with the grain line, then cut out the pieces and transfer the pattern markings (see page 37). Since this is only a mock-up, you could mark them with pen. If the garment is very fitted, mark guidelines on the pattern too – a horizontal line through the bust point and a vertical line down the centre of the pattern.

2   Check everything has been marked and remove the pattern pieces. If there are lots of pieces, label them to avoid confusion.

3   With a contrast thread so you can see the stitching easily, sew the toile using short tacking (basting) stitches – but leave the centre back seam open so you can place the toile on the dress form or model. Hand stitches or a long machine stitch are easier to unpick if you need to make changes.

4   Place the toile on the dress form or model – it's a good idea to try it on inside out, as it's easier to make adjustments to darts and seams. Close the centre back seam – you can just pin it closed.

5   Check the fit – is it too tight or too loose? Does it hang nicely? Is there enough ease for the wearer to move around comfortably? If the position of seam lines needs to be changed, unpick that section and mark the new seam line with a pen. If you need to add at the seam line, patch the opening with a piece of fabric.

6   Line up the bustline on the toile over the point of the bust and check that the vertical lines you marked on the pieces are straight and parallel. Make sure any bust darts point up towards the dart point.

7   Check that the side seam is at right angles to the waistline – if it is being pulled forwards, you might need to adjust the bust (see pages 16–18).

8   Check the length of the bodice below and above the bust. Change the waistline on the toile if necessary. If there is too much or too little fabric above the bustline, check the armhole to see if adjustments need to be made at the side seam or across the front of the bodice. If your toile has sleeves, make all the necessary alterations to the bodice before fitting them.

9   Check all necessary adjustments to the pattern are clearly marked on the toile.

TRANSFERRING ADJUSTMENTS

1   Carefully unpick all the seams and darts on the toile and press it flat.

2   If there are not too many changes, use the toile pieces as a template to redraw darts and seam lines on the original pattern pieces. If you needed to add extra material, cut the pattern open and tape in a new piece; if you removed material, fold and tape the pattern to reflect that (see Making Pattern Adjustments on pages 14–19).

3   If there are lots of changes, it might be quicker to draw new pattern pieces by copying the toile. It would also be a good idea to make a second toile from the new pattern pieces.

4   When you are happy with the fit, use the new pattern pieces to cut out the final fabric pieces.

TOP TIP

If you plan to re-use the same pattern, transfer the markings to sturdy paper or thin card instead of tissue or pattern paper to make more robust pattern pieces that can be used again and again.

A word on dress forms

A dress form (sometimes known as a tailor's dummy or a dress stand) is a full-scale replica of a human body that can be used to drape fabric directly onto, to create original designs without a pattern, or to place the garment onto to check and adjust the fit during any stage of construction. There are a lot of different options, so before buying one it's important to consider exactly what you need it for.

Dress forms can have a papier-mâché frame with padding and a jersey cover, or might have a moulded fibreglass frame covered with either felt or foam, or even be made completely from memory foam, which has properties similar to human tissue. Professional dress forms have a tightly-fitting cover made from a special linen fabric called red-edge linen, which shrinks when wet and moulds to the form. They may also have guidelines for common fitting points, such as the bust, waist, centre back, centre front and shoulders.

As well as different sizes and forms for men, women and children, you will also find several different shapes:

- **Full body** (also known as full bifurcated) – which has arms and separated legs
- **Half body** – upper body from neck down to below the hips but without separated upper legs
- **Full torso** – upper body from neck down to mid-thigh with separated upper legs
- **Lower torso** – hips and upper thighs with separated legs
- **Upper torso** – shoulders and to just above waist
- **Trouser from** (also known as a bifurcated leg form) – waist to ankles with separated legs

The most common shape used for home dressmaking is the half body, although if you plan to make lots of trousers you could find the trouser form useful.

Look for a dress form that it is fully pinnable. This will allow for pins to be fully inserted at any angle, so you can place fabric pieces of the garment in place even before it is sewn together, or drape fabric. A partially pinnable dress form only holds pins placed at an angle, and is mainly used in retail stores for display purposes.

You may be lucky enough to find one that is close to your own body measurements. If not, you can always add padding where necessary. Alternatively a custom dress form is made to measure, created from your own measurements – you can either provide these yourself, or your body is scanned by the company. If you plan to make garments for people of different sizes, there are adjustable dress forms available with dials that can alter bust, waist and hips to match individual measurements.

Professional dress forms are more expensive, but may have additional features:

- Adjustable height.
- Secure metal stand with wheels, which makes it easier to move it around.
- Cage – a metal cage extending below the body for working on long dresses, and also as a visual guide for the hem length.
- Hem marker – a marker on the pole of a top-hanging stand that can be raised or lowered to help achieve a level hem.
- Collapsible shoulders – if you plan to make many form-fitting garments, this feature will enable you to take the garments on and off much more easily. Detachable shoulder caps and detachable arms – and on a trouser form collapsible hips and a detachable left leg – also to help put on and remove garments more easily.

Other possible add-ons include detachable feet and head, bendable arms, detachable calves, and even a removable full belly.

STEPS TO BUYING A DRESS FORM

When researching which type to buy, consider the following:

1 How often you will use the form – do you do a lot of fitting or draping? If not, it may be an unnecessary expense.

2 Take detailed measurements of your body. If the bust, waist and hip fall across several standard measurements you will need to pad the body form, or buy an adjustable one.

3 If you make clothes for other people, an adjustable form may be the best option.

Fabric Types

It may be the colour or the pattern of the fabric that first attracts you, but you also need to consider whether the fibre it's made from is suitable for your garment. If you are working from a pattern, the back of the envelope will give you suggested fabric types.

Cotton

Cotton is often blended with other natural fibres, such as silk or linen, as well as with advanced technological fibres that create specific properties – to make a non-iron fabric for shirts, for instance. There are many different ways to weave cotton yarn, all creating very different fabrics. A twill weave, for example, skips warp threads as it's woven, creating texture and a really durable fabric – denim is a great example. Plain weaves create cloths like ginghams and broadcloths. Cotton can also be woven into different weights and dyed in myriad shades. It is very resilient, so can be given special finishes to improve the body and wear, and is easy to launder and cool on the skin.

Wool

There are two types of woollen fabric: woollen yarn, which is produced when the fleece has been carded and then drawn prior to spinning; and worsted yarn, which is carded, drawn, and combed prior to spinning. Woollen spun fabric is easier to sew with and less expensive than worsted fabric, but not ideal for elegant or fine tailoring, as it doesn't hold its shape as well. Worsted spun fabric has a smother, flatter and more lustrous appearance. It is used to make fabrics like twill and suiting and is considered the ultimate fabric for elegant tailoring. Wool dyes well and can be blended with man-made fibres. It keeps you warm in winter and is naturally water-repellent, so is good for outerwear. However, it frays and pills easily, and holds water and shrinks readily, so is best dry cleaned.

Linen

Spun from the long, waxy fibres of the flax plant, linen has a natural lustre and three times the strength of cotton. It doesn't take dye as well as cotton, so linen is usually a plain colour with the pattern woven into rather than printed onto the fabric. Because it creases readily, people either love or avoid linen. Very cool on the skin, it is an excellent summer fabric.

Silk

Silk is an excellent insulator that evolved to keep the silkworm pupae at an even temperature whatever the outside conditions, so it will keep you cool in summer while providing surprising warmth when needed. It can be woven into richly coloured fabrics from fine chiffons to rich exotic brocades. Silk is a soft, fluid fabric that skims the contours for lingerie and feels wonderful against the skin, but its naturally slippery quality makes it something of a challenge to sew. It also frays and marks easily, so finish the edges with an overlocker (serger) or zigzag stitch after cutting, pin within seam allowances or use weights instead, and avoid unpicking seams.

Crêpe

This refers to any fabric that incorporates twisted fibres to give a crinkled surface and improve drape. Crêpe chiffon is similar to chiffon; the surface of the fabric has the textured look typical of a crêpe but instead it's sheer. Considered harder to sew than chiffon, it's used for special-occasion wear. Wool crêpe has a wonderful drape, making it perfect for dresses and blouses; it's available in light to mid weights. Crêpe is also available in many other fibres, so it's possible to buy crêpe fabric as almost any type of cloth.

Gabardine

A classic suiting fabric, gabardine is a tightly woven twill with a distinctive ribbed pattern and a slight sheen. It is typically made of cotton that holds its shape and does not wrinkle, making it perfect for suits, dresses and macs. The cotton can be blended with various fabrics such as polyester and wool for outwear.

Chambray

This is a soft cotton cloth, woven with dyed warp threads and white filler or weft threads, which creates its distinctive sheen and iridescent effect. It launders well and is really easy to sew with. Use a lightweight version for delicious shirts, dresses and children's clothes, and heavier-weight cloth for shorts or trousers.

Corduroy

This cotton fabric has distinctive stripes called 'wales' that run parallel to the selvedge. The wales come in a variety of widths, from fine needlecord to fat jumbo-cords. Choose a lighter-weight, narrow, ribbed cord for shirts or dresses, and hicker ribbed corduroy for dungarees, trousers and jackets. Corduroy is now available in many cute children's prints.

Denim

Denim was originally designed to make workwear but is now available in many weights and is often blended with other fibres to make a more technical cloth. It's a densely woven fabric, so use a denim needle for heavier-weight denim. Lightweight denim makes fabulous shirts, dresses and children's clothes. Heavier weights are excellent for jeans, shorts and jackets.

Jersey

The word 'jersey' is often mistakenly used to describe most knit fabrics. It's a stable, drapey knit with limited stretch. Single-knit jersey has lengthwise fine ribs on one side with purl knit on the opposite side. Double-knit jersey has lengthwise ribs on both sides. T-shirt material is made from cotton jersey, and jersey can also be used to make wrap dresses, tops, skirts and drapey trousers. Sweatshirt knit has a plain or jersey knit on one side and a brushed, loopy, reverse side – it's the napped, brushed reverse side that makes this knit so distinctive and comfortable to wear.

Velvet

This luxurious pile fabric was traditionally made from silk; nowadays, it is more likely to be cotton or synthetic. The pile of velvet is up to 2 mm ($^1/_{16}$ in.) long – anything longer than that is a velour. The pile means that the fabric has a nap and will look different when viewed from different angles, so be aware of this when laying out pattern pieces. Silk or synthetic velvet has a shiny surface, while cotton velvet has a more matte finish – but all velvet is soft and luxurious, and lovely to wear.

Dupion

Dupion is dense, slubby (knobbly) silk fabric woven from silk. Also known as Indian silk, dupion has a distinctive surface texture that has obvious slubs in the weave. It's a crisp, medium-weight silk that's woven in a myriad of colours and is often shot with a second colour. Synthetic versions are also now available.

Satin

Any fibre, from cotton to silk and polyester, can be woven in a satin weave, but it's most effective using long fibres that have their own sheen, such as silk. It's available in all weights, from slinky charmeuse, to heavy duchesse satin. Satin seams can creep when sewn, so choose patterns without lots of seaming and details. The surface has a pile-like quality that is easily crushed when ironed, and the slight nap means it will look different when seen from different angles. It is a slippery fabric, so is difficult to sew, and frays easily so finish the edges with an overlocker (serger) or zigzag stitch after cutting. It marks easily, so pin within seam allowances or use weights, and avoid unpicking seams.

Lace

Originally hand made using a series of intertwined threads and bobbins, or by embroidering a fine cloth, most modern lace is made by machine. Lace is produced either as a fabric or as narrow trim known as an insertion. A lace insertion is a cost-effective way to add a touch of luxury to a garment. While lace is delicate and needs careful handling, it's more forgiving than you might expect.

Viscose/rayon

Viscose is a type of rayon, a silky synthetic fibre. It has the potential to become more environmentally friendly by reusing or recovering the chemicals used in its production, instead of letting them pollute waterways, and by using wood pulp from regulated sources. Viscose is used in garments with drape and is very popular in the fashion industry.

Polyester

The main component in synthetic fibres is oil, which produces plastic fibres. Polyester is a versatile synthetic, which is often used in combination with natural fabrics to make them crease-resistant. Synthetic fibres are not very breathable but can be engineered to have properties like being waterproof or moisture wicking.

MORE UNUSUAL FABRICS

Jacquard

This fabric is made on an elaborate loom invented around 1802 by Joseph Marie Jacquard to mechanize the production of brocades and damasks. The fabric can be made in any fibre. The production method creates a firm, strong but soft fabric that can have delicate and complex patterns – and since the pattern is woven in it appears on both sides, with the design reversed on the back, so some designs are reversible.

Batik

Batiks are indigenous to Indonesia and Java. Wax is painted onto the parts of the fabric that are to be left uncoloured. The fabric is then dyed and, once fully dried, boiled to remove the wax. This is repeated for each colour, building up the design layer by layer to create elaborate and colourful designs. Contemporary batik may also use different methods of applying the wax or dye, such as spraying, cracking or marbling to achieve different effects.

African wax

A traditional fabric from Africa, with designs that range from distinctive African motifs to wacky contemporary motifs. Wax print was developed in the industrial revolution to industrialise batik printing. Originally wax was used as the resist (to protect sections to be left undyed), but these days it is more likely to be a resin. Some designs are then block printed over the base design to add extra detail. Genuine African wax is never screen printed – a wax print will show the colours on both sides, while a screen print on has colour only on one side. The fabric is robust and colourful and makes very distinctive clothing.

Damask

A rich, tightly woven fabric, with the pattern created by blending weaving techniques with several layers of threads. The lustrous satin weave threads create the pattern over a plain or twill background. Damask originated in China but became a major technique in the Middle East around the city of Damascus – hence the name. It was originally made in silk, but modern versions can be in silk, linen, cotton, or synthetic fibres. The tight weave makes the fabric very strong and durable and the fabric is fully reversible – although the design appears in reverse on the back.

CHANGING THE FABRIC

Many garments can be made in different fabrics, depending on the look you are going for or the garment's intended use – and changing the fabric can create a totally different look. For instance, a loose T-shirt in cotton jersey is a very casual garment, but made in silk it would be perfect for the office, or in brocade it would look elegant at a dinner party. Trousers in stiff cotton would have a firm silhouette, while a light floaty material would allow them to swirl around the body in fluid shapes. Casual trousers with an elasticated waistband and drawstring in a soft, drapey viscose print would be ideal for summer days and nights, while in a decadent sand-washed silk they would be elegant evening pair; in a soft, striped cotton, the same pattern would make perfect pyjama trousers.

If you switch from an opaque fabric to a sheer fabric be aware of the seams – they will show, so better to switch to a French seam (see page 115), which will need a wider seam allowance. You also need to be aware of the garment's ease – which is the extra allowed on the measurements to enable the garment to be worn and moved in comfortably. Something designed to be form fitting in stretchy fabric will have no ease – or even negative ease – so if made in a material with no stretch it would be far too tight to wear.

Tools and Techniques

BASIC SEWING KIT

You don't need lots of tools for sewing – here's a list of the essentials. Any extra tools and gadgets that you may need for specific fabrics or more advanced projects will be listed in that project.

- **Sewing machine** – they range from simple models that do little more than straight and zigzag stitch and maybe an automatic buttonhole, to elaborate machines with lots of fancy embroidery stitches. The projects in this book can all be made with a relatively simple machine
- **Sewing machine feet** – regular, zip and buttonhole feet come as standard with most sewing machines
- **Sewing thread** – buy good-quality, all-purpose polyester thread because cheap thread may break
- **Steam iron and ironing board**
- **Tape measure**
- **Dressmaking pins** – good-quality dressmaking and bridal pins are finer so they don't mark the fabric. Glass-headed pins are easier to remove, but avoid plastic-headed ones as the iron may melt them
- **Scissors for fabric** – you need at least a 20-cm (8-in.) blade for cutting out clothes
- **Seam ripper** for rapidly unpicking stitched seams
- **Small, sharp scissors** for clipping, snipping threads and using at the sewing machine
- **Marking tools** – start with old-fashioned tailor's chalk or a chalk pencil; you'll need a couple of colours
- **Metre rule** – this is useful for straightening off the edge of fabrics and cutting out freehand
- **Curved ruler** for tracing off patterns. If you want to save money buy one that also has a right angle, which is useful when altering patterns

- **Seam allowance gauge** – this little tool can make hemming and all sorts of fiddly measuring a breeze
- **Dressmaker's carbon paper and tracing wheel** – useful for marking up darts and transferring pattern markings
- **Tracing paper** – to trace the patterns in the book
- **Sewing machine needles** – buy a pack or two of multi-sized universal sewing machine needles
- **Hand-sewing needles** – for sewing on hooks and buttons and hand hemming

As you gain more experience, you may also want to invest in a few extra machine feet:

- **Invisible zip foot**
- **Pin-tuck foot** – for sewing neat and even pin tucks
- **Rolled hem foot** – for sewing a very narrow hem on fine fabrics
- **Gathering foot** – for neat and even gathers

When buying, check that they are the correct ones for your machine as each manufacturer's are slightly different.

THREADING

Fill the bobbin with the same thread as you are using in the needle and insert into the machine. Remember to raise the presser foot before threading the needle to ensure the thread slips between the tension discs, then follow the thread path (which is usually numbered). Make sure you add a thread retainer disc to hold the thread spool on the spindle. To bring up the bobbin thread, hold the needle thread end firmly while raising and lowering the needle, which will bring up a loop of the bobbin thread. Pull on the needle thread end to bring the bobbin thread end through to the top.

SEWING MACHINE NEEDLES

There are many different types and sizes of sewing machine needles and the chart will help you choose the right one. Needles for domestic sewing machines are universal, meaning they will fit any sewing machine brand. You will need different kinds of needles for industrial sewing machines, and also different needles for overlockers (sergers). In addition tothe different sizes of needles in the chart, you might also need a ballpoint needle for stretch fabrics, a twin needle for decorative topstitching or finishing hems on knit fabrics, and a topstitching needle.

American needle size	European needle size	Fabric weight	Fabric types
8	60	Very fine	Fine silk, chiffon, organza, voile, fine lace
9	65	Very fine	Fine silk, chiffon, organza, voile, fine lace
10	70	Very fine	Fine silk, chiffon, organza, voile, fine lace
11	75	Lightweight	Cotton voile, silk, muslin, spandex, Lycra
12	80	Standard	Cotton, synthetics, spandex, Lycra
14	90	Medium-weight	Denim, corduroy, multiple layers
16	100	Heavy-weight	Heavy denim, heavy corduroy, leather
18	110	Very heavy	Upholstery fabric, leather
20	120	Extra heavy	Heavy upholstery fabric, thick leather, vinyl

TOP TIP

Be sure to change your sewing machine needle regularly. It simply gets blunt after a while and won't stitch as neatly. Also always use the bobbins intended for your make and model of machine – other bobbins may look the same, but sometimes vary slightly in size so won't run smoothly.

INTERFACING

Interfacing is used to give extra body, shaping and support. It is often applied to the wrong side of facings, collars, lapels, waistbands and cuffs. Do not confuse it with interlining, which is usually thicker and is used in heavy garments such as coats between the main fabric and the lining to give added warmth or bulk.

Interfacing comes in fusible and sew-in forms. It can be non-woven, woven or knit – and it also comes in different weights and in black/charcoal or cream/white. It is important to make the right choice, as this can influence the final look and drape of your garment.

Fusible interfacing

This type has a heat-activated adhesive on one side, so to apply it you just iron in place. It works well on most fabrics - but should be avoided on loose-woven fabrics, as the glue might seep through, and on fabrics that will not tolerate the heat of the iron. It's also not a great option for heavily textured fabrics, because the surface is not smooth enough for the interfacing to bond well. Although it's quick to apply, it is very important to fuse it completely the first time to avoid it 'bubbling' – which cannot be rectified later.

TOP TIP

Use a pressing cloth when applying fusible interfacing – it will protect the main fabric from too much heat.

Sewn-in interfacing

This type of interfacing is sewn to the backing fabric within the seam allowance, so the stitches will not show. Although it is slightly more work to apply it than the fusible type, with some fabrics it is the better option as it will add support without affecting the drape. It's also the best option for loosely woven, heavily textured and heat-sensitive fabrics.

Non-woven interfacing

The most common type of interfacing used in dressmaking, this has no grain and can be cut in any direction without fraying.

Woven interfacing

A more specialized interfacing generally only used on very fine fabrics such as silk. Since it is woven it has a grain line, so take care when cutting and be sure to match the grain lines of the main fabric.

Knit interfacing

This is used with knitted or other stretch fabrics, and its knitted construction means it will match the stretch of the main fabric.

CHOOSING THE WEIGHT AND COLOUR

Interfacing comes in three weights: light, medium and heavy. Generally, it is best to choose a weight that matches your main fabric – so light for a lightweight fabric and so on. If the interfacing is too heavy, it will dominate – although that might be the effect you want for sculptural shapes. Use dark interfacing on dark fabrics, and white or cream on lighter fabrics, otherwise the interfacing may show through. You can also use extra layers of the main fabric as interfacing if it is likely to show – such as with transparent fabrics like chiffon.

APPLYING FUSIBLE INTERFACING

Fusible interfacing has a glue applied to one side, which can be seen as a slightly raised surface that may glisten or shine.

1 Cut interfacing to the size of the pattern pieces. If you are using medium- to heavy-weight fabrics, trim the interfacing to fit inside the stitching line.

2 Place the fabric wrong side up on the ironing board with the interfacing glue side down on top. Cover with a damp cloth.

3 Check the manufacturer's instructions to find out what temperature to set your iron to and whether steam is applicable. Place the iron on top of the press cloth and press down in the same position for 10–15 seconds. Lift the iron, move to an adjacent area and press down again. Repeat until the whole area has been pressed.

4 If the corners of the interfacing can be lifted away, press again until it has completely bonded. Leave to cool completely before working with it.

....

TOP TIP

The actual time to achieve a good bond varies depending on interfacing and fabric weight. Always test on a sample first.

....

APPLYING SEW-IN INTERFACING

This is either hand or machine sewn to the reverse of the main fabric. It is the best choice for fabrics where the heat and moisture would damage the fabric.

1 Use the appropriate pattern piece to cut out the interfacing.

2 Stitch it to the reverse of the main fabric section, just inside the seam allowance.

3 To reduce bulk, trim away excess interfacing, cutting the corners at an angle.

....

TOP TIP

Apply sew-in interfacings to the garment, not the facings, so that they will shadow-proof the seam allowances showing through and help prevent facings from rolling out.

....

Pinning and cutting

Before you can cut out your fabric and begin sewing, you need to temporarily attach the paper pattern pieces to the fabric.

Pinning the pattern in place

If you need to place a piece to the fold, pin the edge that sits on the fold first and then pin out to the corners, spacing the pins about 20 cm (8 in.) apart. Make sure the pins go through both layers of fabric. Keep the pins inside the cutting lines, as they'll damage your scissors if you cut over them.

Weighting down the pattern pieces

Pins will leave marks in very delicate fabrics, so weights might be a better choice. You can use either purpose-made dressmaking weights or something heavy like paperweights or even cans of beans to hold the paper pattern pieces in position. Some people find it helpful to mark around the outline of the pattern pieces with chalk before they cut. Use dressmaking scissors or a rotary cutter with a special self-healing cutting mat.

CUTTING

Place your left hand lightly on the pattern and fabric layers and hold your dressmaker's shears in your right hand (reverse this if you're left-handed). Slide the lower blade under the fabric: the shears should rest on the table top and the fabric should be raised as little as possible. Make smooth cuts, using the full length of the blades where you can; you'll need to use shorter cuts

when cutting curves. When you need to move the blades along, move your left hand along too, to hold the fabric steady.

Cutting around notches

Notches appear as small triangles on the edges of your pattern pieces and are used to match one pattern piece exactly with another; you need to cut around them when you're cutting out your fabric pieces. They can be single, double or even triple triangles, but always cut them as a single unit. Sometimes, you'll even see two sets of notches on the same pattern piece – for example, you might have one notch on the front of a sleeve and two on the back, which you'll need to match to notches on the armhole to ensure that you don't put the sleeve in back to front. Use the tips of your scissors to cut the notches outwards. If you miss one, you can mark the notches by snipping into the seam allowance a little – but don't make the cut too large, or you'll cut beyond your stitchng line and end up with a hole in the fabric.

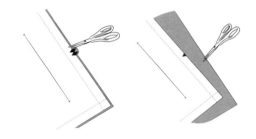

TOP TIPS

- Make sure your fabric is completely flat and wrinkle free when you cut out the pieces.

- If you haven't got a large enough table to cut on, place the fabric on the floor.

- Before you start to cut out, double-check the lay plan(s) to make sure you have all the pieces you need and that they're positioned correctly.

- Iron your paper pattern pieces so that they lie flat.

- Check that the fold lines on the patterns are placed exactly on the fold in the fabric – otherwise the pieces will be slightly too big when cut out.

- Don't lift up the shears or the fabric while you're cutting, as the fabric will shift out of position.

- Don't cut through any fold lines!

Transferring pattern markings

Some pattern markings have to be transferred to your fabric pieces before you remove the paper patterns, as they show where one piece needs to be matched up with another or where to position features such as pockets, darts and zips.

Tailor's chalk and air- or water-soluble markers

These can all be used to add seam allowances, draw in hemlines, mark the position of darts or other features, and mark anywhere where you need to see a stitching line. Always test them on a scrap of your chosen fabric to make sure the lines will brush out or disappear after a wash.

Tracing wheel and dressmaker's carbon paper

Select a colour of carbon paper that will show up on your fabric and position it with the coloured (carbon) side of the paper facing the wrong side of the fabric. Run the tracing wheel around the pattern to produce a line of coloured dots on the wrong side of the fabric.

To mark two identical pieces at once or a piece that's cut on the fold and has symmetrical markings such as darts on both sides, fold your carbon paper in half so that you have the coloured side on both sides, then slot it in between the two layers of fabric. Use your tracing wheel as per usual and mark two lines at the same time.

PIN MARKING

This is a super-useful technique for marking dots and circles on cottons and robust fabrics.

1 Pass a pin through the centre of the circle of the mark you want to transfer. Slide the pin all the way through the pattern and both layers of fabric.

2 Open the two layers of fabric without removing the pin.

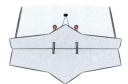

3 Use tailor's chalk or a marking pencil to mark where the pin pricks the fabric. Do the same on the other side of the fabric.

MARKING WITH TAILOR'S TACKS

If you are sewing delicate fabrics, sheers or woollen fabrics on which the chalk/pen marks won't show, mark positions with thread markings called tailor's tacks.

1 Thread a needle with double thread and make a stitch through the circle, through the pattern and both layers of the fabric, leaving at least 2.5 cm (1 in.) thread tail.

2 Make a second stitch at the same spot, leaving a long loop in the stitch. Cut the thread with a long thread tail.

3 Snip into the loop, then gently pull the fabric layers apart and snip the threads in the middle so that some thread is on either side of your pieces.

Edge finishes

If you leave all the raw edges inside your garments unfinished, they will unravel over time, particularly when laundered – and eventually the seams may fall apart. You need to neaten, or 'finish', the seams to prevent this from happening.

USING A ZIGZAG STITCH ON YOUR SEWING MACHINE

If you have a sewing machine with a zigzag function, this is the easiest and most popular way to neaten the edges of your seam allowance. Set the stitch to the widest available, and play around with the stitch length. Start with a 6-mm (¼-in.) width and a 2-mm (⅛-in.) length. Line up the needle so that it 'zigs' inside the fabric and 'zags' next to the edge.

Zigzagging an open seam

When you have an open seam, zigzag both sides of the seam allowance separately.

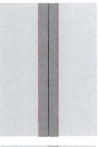

Zigzagging a closed seam

For a closed seam, zigzag the two seam allowances together as one layer.

USING AN EDGE STITCH ON THE SEWING MACHINE

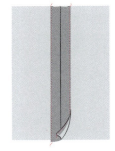

This is a great technique if you have a vintage machine without a zigzag function. Use this technique on open seams only, as it's too bulky for a closed seam. Working from the wrong side of the seam allowance, press under a very narrow fold of about 3 mm (⅛ in.) and stitch with a line of straight stitches. You can fold as you sew, so there's no need for pins.

NEATENING WITH AN OVERLOCKER/ SERGER

An overlocker (serger) is a machine specifically designed to finish the edges and trim in one process, but using a zigzag stitch is just as good for most home sewing. The overlocker has a blade, and if you're new to sewing this can be a little intimidating. An overlocked edge gives a neat, professional finish to your seams.

Reducing bulk

Once you've sewn a seam, you may be instructed to trim, grade, clip or notch the seam allowances to allow the seam to lie flat or sit smoothly on the right side.

Trimming

This is done when the full width of the seam allowance will look bulky on the right side of the garment. It's often done on enclosed seams like a French seam (see page 115). Use sharp scissors to trim away the excess fabric.

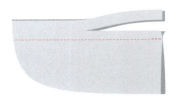

Clipping corners

Where you have stitched around a corner, you need to trim away the bulk before turning it through, otherwise you'll be left with a lumpy, bumpy finish. Trim quite close to the stitching, making sure you don't snip into any stitches. Simply snip off the corner; if it's very pointed, taper the sides well.

Grading

This is done mostly on thick fabric, so that the cut edges inside the seam are staggered. Sometimes only one side of the seam allowance is trimmed away; sometimes both sides are trimmed, but to different depths. It's often done on seams such as flat fell seams.

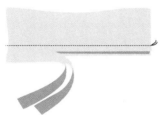

Notching

On an outwardly curved seam, snip triangular wedges along the area of the seam that has the greatest curve, spacing them evenly. On inward curves, such as around a neckline, cut regularly spaced slits into the seam allowance rather than notches.

Machine stitching techniques

There are machine stitching techniques that you'll come across time and time again.

Easing/ease stitch

This is used to gather fabric to ease it into a smaller piece (e.g., when setting in sleeves) or on a curved hem. Increase the stitch length to 4 and sew just inside the seam allowance; on sleeve heads, sew again 3 mm (⅛ in.) from the first row. Pull up the stitching to gather the piece to the required length.

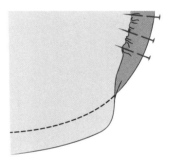

Edge stitching

This is the same as topstitching, but it is sewn much closer to the edge, hence its name.

Gathering

Gathering threads are used to make a longer piece of fabric fit onto a shorter piece. Gathering creates shape in garments, and puts soft pleats or folds along the edge that has been gathered up.

1 Set your sewing machine to a long stitch length – usually about 4 mm (³⁄₁₆ in.). (Your manual should tell you the optimal length on your model.) Working on the right side between the circles, sew a row of stitches inside the seam allowance, a fraction away from the seam line – about 1.2 cm (½ in.) from the edge. Start with a backstitch, but DON'T finish the row of stitches with one. Sew a second parallel row of stitches still inside the seam allowance, a little way from your first row, using the presser foot width as a guide.

2 Working on the wrong side pull on the bobbin threads, sliding the fabric along until it is the correct length. To work out the length, measure your gathered seam against the edge you're matching the gathers to. Once the correct length, draw the threads through to the wrong side and knot them or wrap them around a pin in a figure-of-eight.

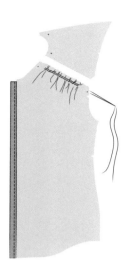

Stay stitching

Stay stitching is done just inside the seam allowance, to prevent bias-cut or curved areas from stretching out of shape while you work on them. Sew with a regular stitch length just inside the seam allowance.

Stitching 'in the ditch'

This is stitching that is done directly on top of a previous seam line, on the right side of the garment. It's a great way to anchor facings or waistbands in place, particularly if they are a heavy fabric that you don't want to turn under. Done well, the stitching disappears inside the crease (or 'ditch') of the seam.

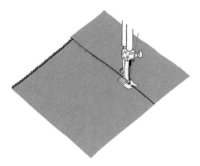

Topstitching

This is stitching that is visible on the surface. Topstitched hems are sewn about 1 cm (⅜ in.) from the edge, or close to the edge on collars and shoulders.

Understitching

This is used to anchor the seam allowance to a facing to prevent the facing from rolling out. Sew the facing to the garment, then press both facing and seam allowances away from the garment. With the facing uppermost, sew close to the seam on the facing, catching the seam allowances underneath as you sew.

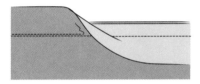

Hems

Whatever method of hemming you use, first you need to prepare the hem allowance.

PREPARING THE HEM ALLOWANCE

The hem allowance adds weight to the hem and helps it hang nicely. An A-line skirt in lightweight cotton needs only a little hem allowance of 2.5–5 cm (1–2 in.), while medium-weight straight skirts, dresses, jackets and trousers (pants) benefit from a hem allowance of up to 8 cm (3 in.).

1 Preferably hang the garment for 24 hours prior to hemming to allow the fabric to settle and even drop if it is cut on the bias. You can then straighten the hem edge before neatening and hemming.

2 Mark the hem level from floor upwards, placing pins parallel to the hem line.

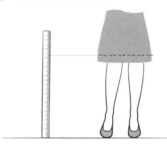

TOP TIP

When marking hem levels, make sure that the person for whom the garment is being made is wearing the appropriate underwear and shoes, as this affects how the garment will hang.

3 Working on a flat surface, with the garment turned wrong side out, fold up the hem at the marked hemline, matching the side, centre back and front seams. Place pins vertically, removing the horizontal pins.

4 Decide on the hem allowance and mark the upper limit. Trim the hem allowance even if necessary.

5 Finish the raw edge of the hem allowance prior to stitching the hem in place by zigzag stitching or overlocking (serging) close to the edge and then trimming close to the stitching. Fabrics that do not fray, such as stretch knits and fleece, do not need to be neatened.

DOUBLE-TURNED HEM

A double-turned hem looks neat and there are no raw edges visible, so it's a strong hemming technique, too.

It can be achieved in two ways. You can either fold up the hem by half the required amount and then again by the same amount, which folds the raw edge under. (However, if your hem is deep, the enclosed edge should be narrower than the hem depth, as this gives a smoother finish.) Alternatively, you can fold up the entire hem allowance and then tuck the raw edge inside.

Press and stitch close to the inner fold of the turned-up hem. Generally you will be working from the wrong side of the garment, so make sure that the bobbin has thread to match the fabric. If desired stitch again, working in the same direction close to the hem edge, to provide two parallel lines of stitching.

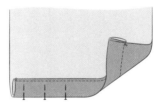

FULL OR CURVED HEMS

On a very full or curved hem, you will have to ease in some of the excess hem allowance before turning up the hem.

1 First prepare the hem allowance (see overleaf).

2 Ease stitch (see page 39) 6 mm (¼ in.) from the raw edge, increasing the stitch length to 4–5. Then gently

pull up the stitching (using the bobbin thread) and turn up the hem allowance. The slight ripples and gathers should be in the hem allowance only, leaving the garment edge smooth and ripple free.

3 Turn the raw edge under, tuck inside the hem allowance and topstitch in place.

PIN HEMMING

This method works really well on curved hems and slippery fabrics. Rather than struggle trying to fold two delicate hems on top of one another, it involves stitching the hem twice.

1 Press under a 1-cm (⅜-in.) fold all the way around the bottom of the piece to the wrong side. Work slowly and use a seam-measuring gauge to get an evenly pressed fold.

2 Using a straight stitch on the machine, sew 3 mm (⅛ in.) from the folded edge. Using sharp scissors, trim away the excess fabric close to the stitch line.

3 Press up the narrow hem you've stitched, so that the raw edges are hidden. Stitch a second line, following the first row of stitches, or 3 mm (⅛ in.) from the outside edge. Press the hem flat.

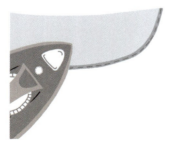

ROLLED HEM

A rolled hem is often used on garments made of sheer or delicate fabrics and is a very narrow hem. It can be sewn on a normal sewing machine (using a special rolled hem foot), by hand or on an overlocker (serger), though the exact details will vary depending on your overlocker. Consult your manual for details and suggestions for the thread tension.

A rolled hem foot has a curved channel in the front that double folds the raw edge under before the needle stitches the hem. This means you don't have to manually press the hem before you sew.

1 Attach the foot and set your machine to a straight stitch with a shorter-than-normal stitch length (2.0). Alternatively set a wide but short-length zig-zag.

2 Make a double 3-mm (⅛-in.) fold along the first 8 cm (3 in.) or so and pin in place. (If your fabric is really delicate and pins would leave a hole, just finger press the fold.)

3 Place your garment under the foot, with the edge of the foot on the outer fold. Lower the presser foot and remove the pin. Sew a few stitches, holding both the bobbin and top threads to stop them from getting tangled up in the stitching.

4 Stop with the needle down in the fabric, then lift the foot. Carefully position the fabric in the curved channel of the foot, then lower the foot again and continue sewing.

Darts

Darts help shape garments to fit over body contours at the bust, hips, through the midriff and at the shoulders. Most darts are V-shaped, with the widest part at the outer edge, tapering to a point in the garment.

1 Mark the dart position and length, then fold the fabric right sides together, so that the marks sit one on top of the other (check by pinning through the layers). Either pin along the stitching line or mark the line with a chalk pencil and then pin at right angles to the dart.

2 Starting at the garment edge, sew towards the point, taking the last two or three stitches in the fold of fabric at the very point. Do not backstitch; instead, leave long thread tails and knot the ends together.

3 Press waist darts towards the centre back of the garment and press bust darts downwards.

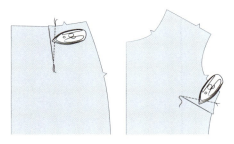

TOP TIPS

○ Bust darts are added to give shape to the bodice, so they need to be pressed carefully to keep the shaping. To do so, press the dart over a tailor's ham (or a rolled towel, or use the end of the ironing board), holding the side seam up as you press into the tip.

○ If you've sewn a single dart on a heavy-weight fabric that would cause a ridge if pressed to one side, cut open the fold of fabric to within 1 cm (⅜ in.) of the tip and press the dart open.

○ If you have a left and a right piece, make sure the darts are the same length and are positioned in exactly the same place on each piece.

Set-in sleeves

Set-in sleeves are the most common type of sleeve and feature in several of the garments in this book. The sleeve head needs to fit into the armhole and curve over the shoulder. To do this, the sleeve head has to be cut larger than the armhole and then gathered or 'eased' to fit. Before you insert the sleeves, stitch, press and finish any seams that intersect the garment's armholes.

1 Finish the raw edges. With right sides together, pin the underarm seam of each sleeve and stitch. Press the seams open. Fold the sleeves in half lengthways and mark the centre top with a pin. At the sleeve heads, run gathering stitches (see page 83) between the marks that you transferred from the pattern piece.

2 Turn the garment inside out and the sleeves right side out. With right sides together, slip the sleeves through the armholes, matching up the notches and matching underarm seams

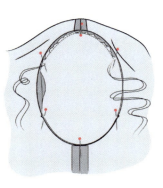

with side seams and the top pin with the shoulder seams. Pin at these points. Gently pull up the gathering stitches to fit the sleeve head in the armhole, arranging the fullness evenly. Tack (baste) the sleeve into the armhole using small stitches, and then stitch in place, beginning and ending at the underarm seam and overlapping the ends of the stitching. Remove the tacking stitches, then trim and neaten the seam allowances. Press the armhole seams towards the sleeve, working the tip of the iron along the curve of the seam.

Facings

Facings are used to neaten and finish off the edges on armholes, necklines and waists, instead of collars, sleeves and waistbands. They are also found on the front openings of many blouses and jackets or coats. They are usually cut from the same fabric as the garment and interfaced to add support. Once attached, a facing is turned to the inside of a garment, so that it is invisible from the outside.

NECK FACING

Regardless of the neckline shape – round, square, sweetheart or V-shape – the construction of a neck facing is much the same. It may consist of a front and back facing, as shown here, or (if the garment has a centre back opening) of one front and two back facings. Sew the shoulder seams of the garment before you attach the neck facing.

1 Apply interfacing to the front and back neck facings. With right sides together, pin the front and back neck facings together at the shoulder seams. Machine stitch.

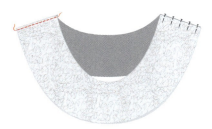

2 Neaten the seam allowances and press the seams open. Neaten the lower edge of the facing with a zigzag stitch or an edge stitch, or on an overlocker (serger).

3 Lay the garment flat, right side up. Lay the facing right side down on top, matching up the raw edges of the neckline and the shoulder seams. Pin, then sew around the neckline. (If the neckline is curved, as shown here, sew slowly and clip the neckline curve (see page 39).

4 Press both the facing and the seam allowances away from the body of the garment. Understitch (see page 40) the facing around the neckline, stitching only through the facing and the seam allowance. Secure the facing to the shoulder seam allowance of the garment with a few small hand stitches.

COMBINED NECK AND ARMHOLE FACING

This is a great way to finish the neckline and armholes of a garment at the same time. It can be used for any sleeveless garment that has a seam at the centre back. Sew the shoulder seams of the garment before you attach the facing.

1 Apply interfacing to the front and back neck facings. With right sides together, pin the front and back neck facings together at the shoulder seams. Machine stitch. Neaten the lower edge of the facing with a zigzag stitch or an edge stitch, or on an overlocker (serger).

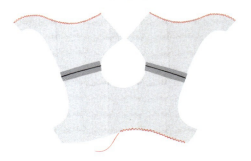

2 Lay the garment flat, right side up. Lay the facing right side down on top, matching up the raw edges of the neckline and the shoulder seams. Pin, then sew around the neckline.

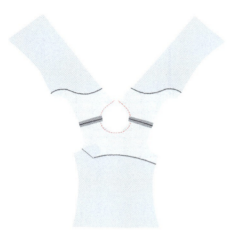

3 If the neckline is curved, as here, clip the neckline curve (see page 39).Press the seam allowances towards the facing and understitch (see page 40) the facing from the right side. Be sure to only stitch through the facing and the seam allowance.

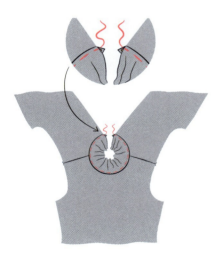

4 Now turn the facing inside out, so that the facing and garment are right sides together. Pin the facing around the armholes and the centre back neck opening, matching the shoulder seams. Machine stitch in place. Clip into the curved armhole seams.

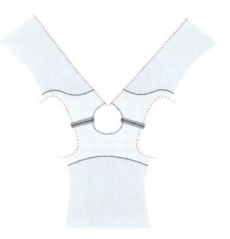

5 Attach a safety pin to one corner of each back piece. Use the safety pin the slide the first back piece through the 'tunnel' at the shoulder, through to the right side. Repeat on the opposite shoulder.

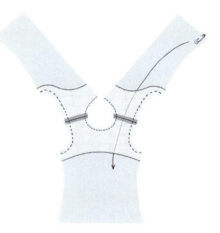

6 From the wrong side, press the facing really flat at the armholes, centre back opening and neckline, rolling the seam lines in towards the wrong side as you press.

7 Place the front and back of the garment right sides together, matching the side seams. Lift up the facing at the side seams and pin and stitch the side seams from the top of the facing through the underarm seam, all the way down to the hem. Press the seams open and turn the facing to the wrong side of the garment. Press the armhole edge. Use a hand stitch to secure the hem of the facing to the side seams.

8 Pin and sew the centre back seam from the hem to the bottom of the facing. Press the seam open. Insert the fastening of your choice into the centre back seam.

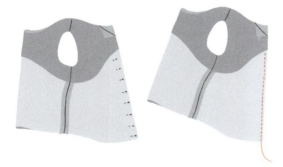

....

TOP TIPS

∘ **A facing should be exactly the same shape as the garment edge that it finishes, so if you alter the shape of the garment in any way (for example, by changing the shape of the neckline), remember to alter the facing to match.**

∘ **Facings are usually interfaced. Choose an interfacing that's the same weight or lighter than the garment fabric.**

....

Applied casing for elastic

An applied casing is created from a separate piece of fabric.

1 To calculate the width of the casing fabric or bias binding, measure the width of the elastic being used and add 12 mm (½ in.) for seam allowances plus 1 cm (⅜ in.) for ease. The casing should be long enough to go around the garment ungathered, plus 3 cm (1¼ in.) to neaten the ends. Cut the casing to this measurement, cutting it on the straight grain if the waistline of the garment is straight and on the bias if it is curved.

2 Turn one long edge of the casing to the wrong side by 6 mm (¼ in.) and press. Press 1 cm (⅜ in.) to the wrong side at each short end and machine stitch.

3 Trim the garment waist seam allowance to 1 cm (⅜ in.) With right sides together, starting near a seam, pin the un-pressed edge of the casing all the way around. Stitch in place.

4 Press, then flip the casing to the wrong side of the garment. Pin and stitch the lower edge of the casing in place.

5 Insert the elastic following steps 3 and 4 of Fold-down casing for elastic (page 197). Slipstitch the edges of the casing together, making sure you don't catch the elastic in the stitching.

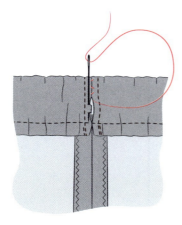

Conventional zip, centred

This is the simplest form of zip insertion; the zip sits in the centre of the zip opening. Overlock (serge) or zigzag the seam allowances before you insert the zip.

1 Machine tack (baste) the seam of the garment. For a garment that has a zip inserted partly into a seam, such as a dress or a skirt, sew up the seam from the hem to the zip notch on a normal stitch length, backstitch, then machine tack the rest of the seam. Press the seam allowances open.

2 Place the garment wrong side up, with the zip face down on the seam and the zip teeth in the middle of the seam. Pin in place, inserting the pins horizontally. If you need a fastening such as a hook and bar or if a waistband is going to be attached, make sure that the zip head lies 1.5 cm (⅝ in.) below the raw edge.

3 Fit a regular zip foot to your machine. Turn the garment over and pin the zip in place from the right side in a U-shape, in the direction you're going to sew. The foot needs to sit next to the zip so that you can stitch close to it. On some machines the zip foot is static and you change the needle position; on others, you can unclip the foot and position it to the left or the right of the needle. Indicate where you want to cross over the bottom of the zip to sew the other side. Mark this with a pin just above the zip stopper.

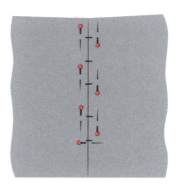

4 Remove the pins from the wrong side of the zip and start stitching from the top. Pivot and stitch across the bottom, then pivot again and stitch the other side.

5 Unpick the tacking stitches from step 1: your zip should now sit beautifully in the centre of the seam.

Buttons and buttonholes

Badly stitched buttonholes ruin any garment, so the key is to practise on spare fabric. Make up the layers of fabric as they appear on the garment (usually a folded piece) so that you can test the buttonhole setting on your sewing machine. First, however, you'll need to mark the buttonhole positions.

POSITIONING BUTTONHOLES AND BUTTONS

The centre front of your buttoned-up garment will lie somewhere along the middle of the button stand (the area of the garment that holds the buttons on one side and the buttonholes on the other). This should be indicated on your pattern. When you overlap the button stands, the centre front lines will lie on top of each other. The buttons and buttonholes will be positioned along this line.

- Buttons go on top of the centre front line.
- Horizontal buttonholes should start 3 mm (⅛ in.) from the centre line towards the edge of the garment.
- Vertical buttonholes go on top of the centre line.

Sewing patterns are usually marked with the buttonhole positions, but if yours is not or you want to change the positions to some that are more flattering to your figure, measure and mark them carefully. Buttonholes should be at least 1–2 cm (⅜–¾ in.) from the fabric edge and 5–8 cm (2–3 in.) apart, depending on the fabric weight and style of the garment.

Use a sewing gauge to check your positioning. Use the sliding marker to ensure all the buttonhole positions are evenly spaced and at exactly the same position in from the edge of the opening.

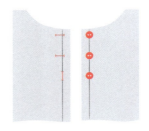

STITCHING BUTTONHOLES

Modern machines will either sew a buttonhole in one step or, on basic models, in four steps. Many now come with a buttonhole foot with a slot in the back for the button, so that the hole is the perfect size.

Prepare the fabric by interfacing the buttonhole section. On very lightweight fabrics, add an extra layer of tearaway stabilizer below each buttonhole area.

Buttonhole foot with slot for button

1 Insert the button into the back of the foot, following the manufacturer's instructions.

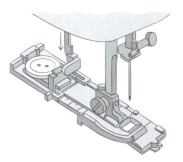

2 Snap on the buttonhole foot and bring down the buttonhole lever. Set the sewing machine to your chosen buttonhole stitch, which is usually a one-step buttonhole when this foot is supplied.

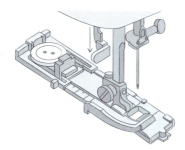

3 Position the garment under the foot, with the needle ready to insert into the correct end of buttonhole placement mark (which end of buttonhole depends on which way your machine stitches). Once stitched, feed the thread tails through to the back of the work and then through the close stitching of one side before cutting them off.

4 Place a pin at one end of the buttonhole so that you don't accidentally cut through the end bar. Starting at the other end, use a seam ripper or a pair of small, sharp scissors to open the buttonhole.

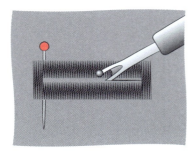

Four-step buttonhole

1 Attach the buttonhole foot and select step 1 of the buttonhole sequence. (You may need to adjust the stitch length down to virtually 0, too.) Stitch the first end bar tack. Once complete, the machine will stop ready for you to turn the dial to step 2 to stitch the left side of the buttonhole.

2 Stitch the length needed, stopping at the marked line you made for your buttonhole size. Turn the dial back to step 1 for the second bar tack. Then turn the dial to stitch the right-hand side, stitching until you reach the first bar tack. Take threads to the back and tie off. Open the buttonhole, as in step 4 to the left.

Tips and Troubleshooting

Beginner or confident sewer, we can all do with a few tips to make our sewing journeys easier. These tips, many of which can be developed into sewing habits, have the potential to improve your sewing workflow and save you time and stress. We've also included solutions to some common sewing problems.

PRIOR TO SEWING

Make a note of your body measurements

The sizes on sewing patterns differ from pattern to pattern and may not be the same as standard sizes, so get your measurements correct before cutting the patterns out – see Measuring on page 12.

Sew a toile

It's tempting to launch straight into cutting up your fabric using the body size chart on your sewing pattern sheet – but creating a toile (see page 24) first, before cutting up your final fabric, is invaluable.

Take your time over pattern adjustments

If your garment wrinkles or puckers around or below the bust, an adjustment needs to happen. The fit of your garment relies on the shoulders and armholes matching up with your body; the armhole should fit smoothly without gaps or strain, while the shoulder seam should align with your natural shoulder line. The sleeve should feel non-restrictive and allow ease of movement. If these areas, or the waist and hips, do not fit well, adjust the pattern pieces (see pages 14–19).

Label your pattern pieces

Label pattern pieces using a lightly sticky tape – especially top and under collars, facings, outer and inner facings, and left- and right-hand sides of wrap-style garments – so that you can identify them quickly.

Make sure your marks will last!

When transferring pattern markings, ensure that the method you choose will last through all the garment construction but will be easy to remove on completion. If an important mark gets rubbed off during the sewing process, have your original sewing pattern at hand so that you can re-mark it. Test your marking method on a swatch of your fabric first – particularly with erasable markers, as they can indelibly mark some fabrics.

WHILE SEWING

Leave long thread tails

Always leave a tail about 13 cm (5 in.) long on both bobbin and top threads as you begin sewing to avoid tangles. Push these thread tails towards the back of the sewing machine and held in the direction of sewing, avoid tangles at the beginning of a line of stitching.

Sew a test swatch

Take a moment to sew a test scrap at the beginning of a project to check stitch lengths and thread tensions.

Follow the instructions!

Do not ignore any stay stitching instructions (see page 40). Stay stitching helps the curved edge of a fabric to keep its shape and not stretch while sewing.

Add interfacing where necessary

Interfacing adds extra support to your fabric, especially in areas like facings and collars (see page 34). Take time to choose the right interfacing for the fabric type you are working on.

Work in sections

Work on your garment in sections, with all the smaller parts stitched into sections before they get coupled together. For instance, cuffs should be stitched onto sleeves and collars attached to bodices before they are attached to each other.

Hang before hemming

Hemming a garment is usually one of the last steps on most sewing pattern instructions. But one thing that is easy to skip is to hang the garment overnight before hemming it. This allows gravity to shape the garment – especially with drapier fabrics or garments cut on the bias. Garments that include linings should always be hung overnight to ensure that the main and lining fabrics take shape together – then, if they do not hang the same way, adjustments can be made in advance. After hanging, mark the hem with the garment on the body, then trim it on a flat surface (see page 40).

TROUBLE SHOOTING

Sewing machine gets tangled up when stitching

When your machine is not creating stitches the way it should, remove the upper and bobbin threads and then carefully re-thread the sewing machine. This should help the machine to stitch properly again.

Machine stitches are irregular

The top tension may be too loose, so try adjusting it and test on a scrap of fabric. Another possibility is incorrect presser foot pressure; check you have it on the correct pressure for the fabric you are sewing. Or you may simply be pulling the garment through the machine faster than it is stitching – you should only be guiding the fabric through.

Skipped stitches

This may be due to a blunt needle, so change to a fresh one. Or the machine may be incorrectly threaded, in which case re-thread from scratch. Or you may be using the wrong needle/thread for your fabric.

Thread looping or bunching underneath the fabric

This is probably a threading problem – either the machine is not threaded correctly, or the top tension is too loose. Try rethreading and adjusting the top tension, then test on a scrap of fabric. If there is still a problem, the needle may be the wrong type for the thread being used (see page 34 for the correct needle weight for different fabric types).

Seams are puckering

You may be using a stitch length that is too long for the fabric being sewn – so you are basically sewing gathering stitches without meaning to. Alternatively the top tension is incorrect, or the top thread is not threaded properly, in which case rethread and adjust the top tension, then test on a scrap of fabric. Check you have the right needle in the machine and it is not blunt. Another possible cause is that the thread in the top and in the bobbin don't match – always use the same weight and type of thread in both places.

Needle is pushing the fabric into the needle plate

This sometimes happens with very fine fabrics – you may need to stabilize the fabric with tissue behind it while you sew. It could also be caused by a blunt or incorrect needle.

Top thread breaks

First check the thread quality – old or cheap thread may not be suitable for machine sewing, or it may have a knot that is catching on the needle. Another possibility is that the machine is threaded incorrectly, or the top tension is too tight; rethread and adjust the top tension, then test on a scrap of fabric. Make sure you are using the right needle for the thread and fabric, and that the needle is not blunt.

Bobbin thread breaks

You may be using the wrong type of bobbin for the machine, or the bobbin has not been fully and properly inserted. Check you have the right bobbin and rethread the bobbin thread. Another possibility is that lint has built up around the bobbin case or under the feed dogs, in which case clean the machine with the small brush provided.

Sustainable Sewing

Sewing and sustainability can go hand in hand – we can all make sustainable choices when selecting fabric, buttons, zips and threads. Use up what you have, wear what you make, and make informed choices about the rest.

Buying sustainable fabrics

If you want your fabric purchases to be more sustainable, here are some questions to ask yourself:

- Can I trace the origin of this fabric? Look for fabrics that clearly display their place of origin.

- Was the crop for this fabric farmed in a regulated or organic way? Low use of pesticides is better for the planet as well as for the workers.

- Did this fabric travel far to reach me? Air miles have a high environmental impact.

- Is this fabric made of natural or synthetic fibres? Natural fibres are a more sustainable choice, as they are biodegradable.

- How impactful is the crop that this fabric was made from? Cotton, for example, has a high environmental impact due to its high water usage, whereas linen has a much lower water usage.

- Can I use up fabric I already have at home rather than buying new?

Printed and dyed fabrics

Look for certification of the chemicals used: this ensures that the production of your fabric didn't harm the people working with it or will not cause harm through the wastewater left over after production. Up to 10% of fabric dyes are washed away in the wastewater during the process.

Digital printing is different from dyeing in that it prints a design on the surface of the base material, rather than dyeing the fibres by soaking. Digital printing uses very little to no water and is the most environmentally friendly way of achieving printed textiles.

Thread

Thread is often made of 100% polyester, but other options include organic cotton thread, silk and even thread made from 100% recycled plastic bottles. The plastic cones that your thread is often wrapped on can sometimes be recycled at dedicated recycling points.

Buttons

There is a wide variety of alternatives to plastic buttons, including wooden, shell, resin and vintage buttons. We all have a bag of old buttons in our sewing box and you can often find them at car boot sales and in second-hand shops. Another eco-friendly alternative is the corozo button. Corozo is a 100% natural product similar in consistency to a hard resin.

Zips

Zips tend to be made with plastic and polyester tape, which end up in landfill. A great alternative is to use zips with metal teeth. Not only do they look great, they also come in a variety of metals such as gold, silver and brass. Metal zips are often made with cotton tape and 100% organic cotton zips are becoming more readily available. You can also source plastic zips made from recycled materials.

Sewing patterns

Having made something once, you may not want to use the same pattern again. However, you may be able to re-use old patterns by combining pieces from different ones to make something entirely new.

Offcuts

Lay pattern pieces out as close together as possible, without distorting the grain or the print – this enables you to use the least amount of fabric, leaving you with fewer or bigger offcuts, which are more useful. Cutting on the fold is not always the most economical method: by cutting on a single layer you can usually save some fabric – sometimes even up to half a metre (yard). This will also save you money.

Re-use offcuts

Some offcuts are big enough for baby clothes, or smaller homeware projects and accessories such as bags, hair scrunchies and headbands. You can also turn sizeable offcuts into a new material by patchworking them together.

Re-using fabric

Although we wouldn't want to cut up a gorgeous vintage piece, a damaged garment made of fabulous, no-longer-available fabric can be given a new lease of life. You can either cut out garment pieces from the fabric as you would new fabric, or make use of more complicated parts of the garment construction, such as a collar, sleeve or neckline section. Repurpose items that you no longer wear: you can turn a man's shirt into a blouse, bed sheets into a dress, jeans into a pinafore.

Donating

You can donate your fabric remnants and scraps to local schools or colleges that run art and fashion courses, which is invaluable to the students. Some charity shops take fabric scraps to sell as stuffing for craft projects or to sell to keen quilters. Charity shops, of course, also take unwanted items of clothing – but only donate items that you know can be sold, as the rest will be sold on, often to countries around the world with poor economies. You can also donate clothing to women's shelters, as they are among many other organizations that need clothing.

Fabric and clothing swaps

Fabric swaps are becoming ever more popular within the sewing community, either mini swaps with your friends or large-scale fabric swaps at sewing meet-ups and events. If you would like to organize your own fabric swap, you can create an event on social media or email your favourite sewing bloggers to spread the word. You can also put on a clothing swap, which is another fantastic way to reduce fabric and clothing waste. Many high-street stores also now take your unwanted clothes to be recycled. This process can't always be traced, so also check your local rubbish collection provider to see if they recycle textiles.

....

TOP TIP

Make a tag for any fabrics you want to swap describing what the fabric composition is (for example, 100% viscose), as well as the length and width of the piece.

....

Some sustainable fabric options

There are sustainable options available for makers who are interested in learning more about the impact of their fabric choices. Some materials are brand new and others are some of the oldest fabrics known to mankind.

Abaca

This fibre comes from the abaca tree, a relative of the banana tree that doesn't bear fruit. This relatively newly developed fibre is durable, strong and very breathable.

Bamboo

Bamboo is a very sustainable crop, as it's very hardy against diseases and very fast growing. Select an organic or closed-loop production to ensure the production takes care of the chemical components needed to turn the pulp into fibres.

Ethical silk

Also called peace silk or ahimsa silk, this is made by silkworms that have been allowed to mature into butterflies. The process does not harm the insects and takes much longer to make than regular silk.

Hemp

Hemp production uses around 3% of the water that cotton production uses and yields the biggest harvest of all natural fibres.

Hessian

Known as burlap in the US and Canada and as crocus in Jamaica, this fabric is made from jute, a plant fibre that's very strong, versatile and affordable. Growing jute purifies the air and the crop grows very quickly. It's often used to make sturdier fabrics but can also be combined with other fibres to produce more lightweight versions.

Kapok

Made from the kapok tree and traditionally used as a filling material, this cellulose fibre is very silky and soft to the touch and is hypoallergenic, making it suitable for bedding. Kapok is blended with other fibres to create a fabric, as it cannot be used on its own.

Linen

The fibre that linen is woven from, flax, is a much less thirsty crop than cotton and it grows in Europe, too. If you are based in Europe, this means that the fabric hasn't travelled as far, reducing the air miles between the crop and your doorstep.

Pina

This is made from the leaves of the pineapple plant, which can be turned into a fabric. It can be combined with other fibres to create a very lightweight fabric.

Piñatex

This is an innovative alternative to leather made from pineapple leaves, mostly used in vegan shoes and bags that are made to look like leather.

Ramie

Ramie is a flowering plant in the nettle family. It is similar to cotton and linen in weight and weave, but much more durable as a material and the crop is very sustainable to grow.

Tencel

Also known as Lyocell, Tencel is a cellulose fabric made from the wood pulp of trees. It is produced in an environmentally friendly way and certified closed loop. All resources are used at maximum capacity rather than going to waste, leaving a low ecological impact.

Sustainable laundry & dry cleaning

When you have made your new clothes, another important step towards a more sustainable wardrobe is how you care for them. The first thing to think about is how often you wash and at how many degrees. Clothes last longer if they are washed at 20–40°C and this is a more environmentally friendly way to wash than a hotter wash, which you can reserve for bed linens and towels if really necessary. Clothes actually respond better to these washing cycles, as hotter temperatures usually damage the fibres and therefore shorten the lifespan of your garments. Make sure that you wash a full load to make full use of the water.

Sometimes it's only parts of a garment that really need cleaning, so you could consider spot cleaning or a hand wash.

Use a detergent that has a reduced amount of chemicals in it, which includes synthetic fragrances. These detergents are less harmful to the planet's waterways and are a relatively easy way to reduce your laundry's impact. You can also consider making your own. There are also some great tips online.

Getting rid of stains

Garments made from synthetic fibres, such as polyester, nylon and fleece, contain micro plastics. These are very small particles that are released when submerged in water during a laundry cycle and are washed out into the waterways with the wastewater from the washing machine. There are currently only a limited number of ways to catch these microfibres to keep them out of seas, rivers and oceans, but they do exist. In the near future, there will hopefully be many more solutions.

· ·

TOP TIP

After you have done your laundry, consider air drying rather than tumble drying to conserve energy. If you have to dry clean your clothes, look for a dry-cleaning company that eliminates the use of a chemical called percholorethylene, which is the most harmful of all the chemicals used in dry cleaning.

· ·

The Projects

'Paperbag' Waists

Paperbag waists (so called because, when belted, they look a bit like a scrunched-up paper bag that you're holding by its neck) are a high-rise style that's cinched in around the slimmest part of the waist, with extra fabric sticking out above the belt or tie. The waist style adds a frilly touch to an otherwise workaday pair of shorts or trousers and, because there's a good amount of volume around the middle, tends to look best paired with a close-fitting top or shirt.

Paperbag Shorts

These shorts have only small amount of fabric above the waist, creating a fairly streamlined look, but you could make the waist casing deeper so that it extends further above the waist if you prefer a more ruffled look. The legs are baggy, but the turn-ups create a more tailored finishing touch.

Materials

- Sizes 8–14: 1.7 m (1⅞ yd) fabric, 150 cm (60 in.) wide
  Sizes 16–22: 2 m (2¼ yd) fabric, 150 cm (60 in.) wide

- 2 m (2¼ yd) elastic, 3 cm (1¼ in.) wide

- Basic sewing kit (see page 32)

Difficulty level

Intermediate

Fabric suggestions

Cotton, chambray, viscose, crepe, linen

Design notes

Use a 1.5-cm (⅝-in.) seam allowance throughout, unless otherwise stated. .

Finished garment measurements	8	10	12	14	16	18	20	22
Waist (cm)	90	95	100	105	110	115	120	125
Waist (in.)	35½	37½	39½	41½	43¼	45¼	47¼	49¼
Hip (cm)	105	110	115	120	125	130	135	140
Hip (in.)	41½	43¼	45¼	47¼	49¼	51¼	53¼	55¼
Shorts inside leg (cm)	10	10	10	10	10	10	10	10
Shorts inside leg (in.)	4	4	4	4	4	4	4	4
Trousers inside leg (cm)	74	74	74	74	74	74	74	74
Trousers inside leg (in.)	29	29	29	29	29	29	29	29

CUTTING GUIDE

150 cm (60 in.) wide fabric

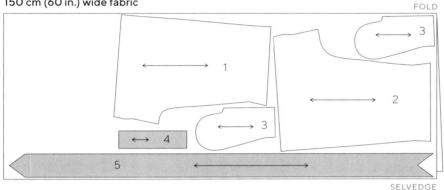

FOLD

SELVEDGE

1 Front – cut 1 pair

2 Back – cut 1 pair

3 Pocket bag – cut 2 pairs

4 Belt loops – cut 1

5 Sash – cut 1

6 Elastic template – do not cut

THE SEWING STARTS HERE

Prepare the pieces

1 Lay out the pattern pieces as shown in the cutting guide. Cut out and transfer any markings to the fabric (see page 37). Be sure to transfer the fold lines for the turn-ups and the waist casing.

Sew the shorts

2 Finish the raw edges of the fronts, backs and pocket bags. With right sides together, pin and sew the front pieces along the centre front seam. Press the seam open. Repeat with the back pieces.

3 With right sides together, matching the notches, pin a pocket bag to each side of the front shorts. Taking an 8-mm (⁵⁄₁₆-in.) seam allowance, sew from the top of the pocket bag to 1 cm (³⁄₈ in.) from the bottom. Press the pocket bags and seam allowances away from the shorts.

4 Repeat step 3 with the back pieces and pocket bags.

5 On the front pieces only, understitch (see page 40) the pocket bag, again stopping 1 cm (³⁄₈ in.) from the bottom. Remember that you're only stitching through the pocket bag and seam allowances.

6 Place the front and back pieces right sides together, matching up the pocket bags. Pin, then sew around the long curved edges of the pockets. (You'll have to move the pocket bag seam allowances out of the way in order to get to the 1-cm (⅜-in.) section that you left unstitched at the bottom of the pocket bags.)

7 Keeping the shorts right sides together, pin the side seams. Stitch from the top edge down to the top of the pocket opening, then from the end of the pocket bag down to the hem. Press the seam and pocket bag towards the front of the shorts.

8 With right sides together, pin and sew the inside leg seams. Press the seams open.

Sew the turn-ups

9 Stitch the turn-ups (see Special Technique: Sewing Turn-ups, page 65).

Stitch the belt loops

10 Cut the belt loop into five pieces, as marked on the pattern. Fold each belt loop in half along the dashed line, matching the raw edges. Stitch along the long edge. Turn right side out and press so that the seam is in the middle of the piece.

11 Press each short end to the wrong side by 6 mm (¼ in.). Referring to your pattern for the positioning, pin the belt loops in place, then stitch across the top and bottom edges of each one, as close to the fold as possible. (There's one belt loop at the centre back, one on each side of it, and two on the front.)

Stitch the waist casing

12 In this pattern the waist casing is part of the shorts, not a separate piece. It is folded over to the inside of the shorts to create a channel; the fold line is marked on the pattern. With the shorts right side out, fold the waist casing to the wrong side and press. Pin the casing in place. Starting at the centre back and stitching 2 cm (¾ in.) below the fold, stitch all the way around, catching the tops of the belt loops in your stitching again to reinforce them.

13 Cut your elastic to the length of the elastic template. Overlap the ends by 1 cm (⅜ in.) and zigzag stitch across the width of the elastic to create a loop. Tuck the elastic inside the waist facing and push it up to the line of stitching that you did in step 12.

14 Pin the elastic to the shorts at the centre back, centre front and side seams. (You will have to stretch it slightly to do so.) Starting at the centre back and referring to your pattern for the stitch line, stitch all the way around, catching the bottoms of the belt loops in your stitching. Try not to catch the elastic in the stitching.

Make the sash

15 With right sides together, fold the sash in half widthways. Press, then pin to hold. Starting from one short raw end, stitch almost to the middle of the long side. Leave a 10-cm (4-in.) gap, then continue stitching to the other end.

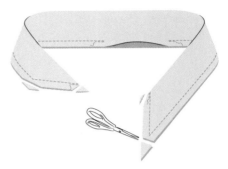

16 Clip the corners (see page 39), then turn the sash right side out through the gap. Turn under the raw edges of the gap, then press the sash. Slipstitch the gap closed.

17 Press the shorts, then thread the sash through the belt loops.

SPECIAL TECHNIQUE: SEWING TURN-UPS

1 Zigzag stitch the raw edge of each leg to neaten it.

2 On your pattern, you'll see three fold lines at the bottom of the legs: the shorts or trouser hemline (the top line), the turn-up fold line (the centre line) and the turn-up hemline (the bottom line). With the shorts or trousers right side out, fold the centre fold line to the wrong side and press.

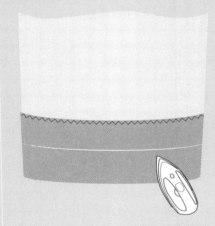

3 Fold the turn-up hemline under by 1 cm (⅜ in.), then stitch in place 6 mm (¼ in.) from the folded edge. Press.

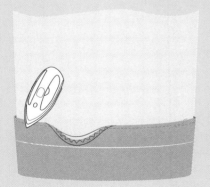

4 Turn the leg right side out. Fold the turn-up along the shorts or trouser hemline and press.

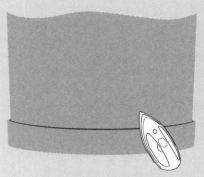

5 Pin the turn-up in place at the side and inside leg seams, then stitch vertically down the turn-up, stitching over the previous seam stitching – in other words, stitching 'in the ditch'. Alternatively, hand stitch the sides of the turn-up to the seams to secure.

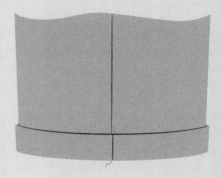

VERSION 2

Paperbag Trousers

This is simply a longer version of the Paperbag Shorts pattern on page 60. The relaxed fit makes the trousers ideal for loungewear.

Materials

- Sizes 8–14: 2.5 m (2¾ yd) fabric, 150 cm (60 in.) wide
  Sizes 16–22: 2.6 m (2⅞ yd) fabric, 150 cm (60 in.) wide

- 2 m (2¼ yd) elastic, 3 cm (1¼ in.) wide

- Basic sewing kit (see page 32)

Difficulty level

Intermediate

Fabric suggestions

Cotton, chambray, viscose, crepe, linen

Design notes

Use a 1.5-cm (⅝-in.) seam allowance throughout, unless otherwise stated.

CUTTING GUIDE

1   Front – cut 1 pair

2   Back – cut 1 pair

3   Pocket bag – cut 2 pairs

4   Belt loops – cut 1

5   Sash – cut 1

6   Elastic template – do not cut

THE SEWING STARTS HERE

1   Lay out the pattern pieces as shown in the cutting guide. Cut out and transfer any markings to the fabric (see page 37). Be sure to transfer the fold lines for the waist facing and turn-ups.

2   Sew the trousers, following steps 2–17 of the Paperbag Shorts (pages 61–64).

150 cm (60 in.) wide fabric

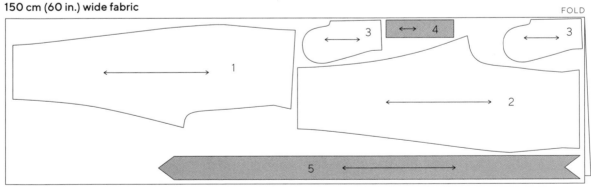

FOLD

SELVEDGE

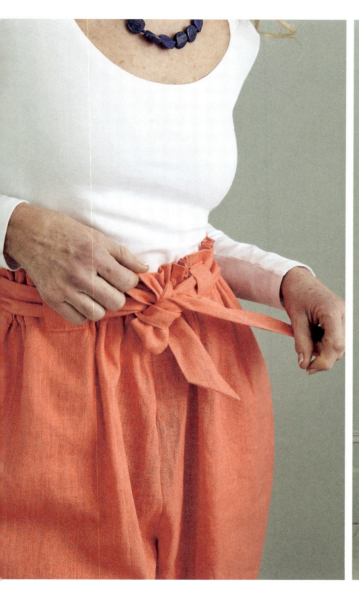

Wrap-over Skirts and Bodices

Wrap-over bodices are flattering to almost all figures – although you may need to alter the dart width or make some other bust adjustment to avoid ending up with a gaping crossover (see page 16). Your choice of fabric will greatly influence the final look: a heavier fabric such as a wool mix or tweed will make a wrap-over skirt look crisp and tailored, while a thin cotton is far more informal and floaty. Before you sew any wrap-over section in place, remember to tack (baste) it in place to check the fit.

Wrap Dress

Figure-hugging and flattering, this dress has both a wrap-over bodice and a wrap-over skirt – though you could ring the changes by substituting a more fitted A-line skirt or a non-wrap V-necked bodice, as in the Pleated Dress on page 134. Made here in a mid-weight patterned Jacquard fabric that drapes beautifully, it is both stylish and elegant, yet not too formal.

Materials

- 3 m (3⅜ yd) fabric, 150 cm (60 in.) wide
- 40 cm (16 in.) lining fabric, 150 cm (60 in.) wide
- 70 cm (28 in.) interfacing
- 56-cm (22-in.) invisible zip
- Basic sewing kit (see page 32)
- Turning tool (optional)
- 2.5-cm (1-in.) wide slider buckle

Difficulty level

Confident sewer

Fabric suggestions

Linen, jacquard, denim, crepe, viscose, sateen

Design notes

Use a 1.5-cm (⅝-in.) seam allowance throughout, unless otherwise stated.

Finished garment measurements	8	10	12	14	16	18	20	22
Bust (cm)	84.5	89.5	94.5	99.5	104.5	109.5	114.5	119.5
Bust (in.)	33¼	35¼	37¼	39¼	41¼	43¼	45	47
Waist (cm)	69	74	79	84	89	94	99	104
Waist (in.)	27	29	31	33	35	37	39	41
Hip (cm)	97	102	107	112	117	122	127	132
Hip (in.)	38	40	42	44	46	48	50	52
Sleeve length (cm)	31.5	32	32.5	33	33.5	34	34.5	35
Sleeve length (in.)	12¼	12½	12¾	13	13¼	13½	13½	13¾
Front length (cm)	110.5	111	111.5	112	113	113.5	114	114.5
Front length (in.)	43½	43¾	44	44¼	44½	44¾	45	45
Back length (cm)	110	110.5	111	111.5	112	112.5	113.5	114
Back length (in.)	43¼	43½	43¾	44	44¼	44½	44¾	45

CUTTING GUIDE

150 cm (60 in.) wide fabric

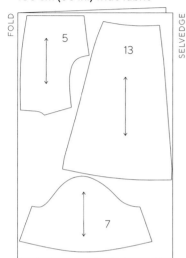

Interfacing

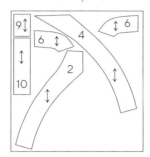

Lining

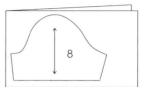

Single layer

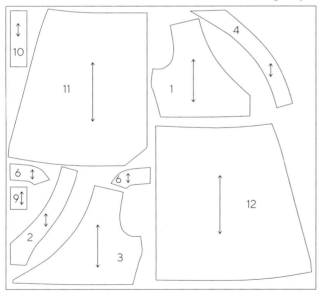

1 Right front bodice – cut 1

2 Right front neck facing – cut 1 in fabric and 1 in interfacing

3 Left front bodice – cut 1

4 Left front neck facing – cut 1 in fabric and 1 in interfacing

5 Back bodice – cut 1 pair

6 Back neck facing – cut 1 pair in fabric and 1 pair in interfacing

7 Sleeve – cut 1 pair

8 Sleeve lining – cut 1 pair

9 Buckle tab – cut 1 in fabric and 1 in interfacing

10 Belt – cut 1 in fabric and 1 in interfacing

11 Right front skirt – cut 1

12 Left front skirt – cut 1

13 Back skirt – cut 1 pair

THE SEWING STARTS HERE

Prepare the pieces

1 Lay out the pattern pieces as shown in the cutting guide. Cut out and transfer any markings to the fabric (see page 37).

2 Following the manufacturer's instructions, apply interfacing to the wrong side of the buckle tab, belt and neck facings (see page 35).

3 Stay stitch (see page 40) the front and back necklines and their corresponding facing pieces.

Construct the bodice

4 Pin and sew the bust darts in the front bodice (see page 42). Press the darts down towards the waistline.

5 With right sides together, pin and sew the front bodices to the back bodices at the shoulders. Finish the seam allowances and press the seams open.

6 With right sides together, fold the belt in half lengthways and sew along the long raw edge. Position the seam allowance in the middle of one side, then press. Pin and sew across one short end. Turn the belt right side out, using a blunt object such as a knitting needle to poke out the corners, and press. Repeat with the buckle strap.

7 Following the marking on the pattern, pin the buckle strap to the right side of the left bodice; the strap should point inwards, away from the side edge of the bodice. Edge stitch the strap in place, then sew a second line of stitches 6 mm (¼ in.) away from the first to ensure the strap stays put.

8 Slide the buckle onto the buckle strap, then fold the other short edge of the strap over, concealing the raw edge, and pin in place. Sew as close to the edge as possible. When overlapped, the left right bodice will conceal the stitching.

9 On the side edge of the right bodice front, find the two notches that mark the position of the belt. With right sides together, aligning the raw edges, pin and tack (baste) the belt to the right side of the right-hand bodice; the belt should point inwards, away from the side edge of the bodice.

10 Finish the raw waistline edges of the front and back bodice pieces.

11 With right sides together and notches matching, pin and sew the back skirt pieces to the corresponding back bodice pieces at the waistline. Press the seams open. Insert the invisible zip (see page 155). The bottom portion of the dress will be open at the centre back. Pin the back pieces right sides together and stitch from the hem to the last zip stitch, then press the seam open.

Attach the facings

12 With right sides together pin the facings together at the shoulder edges. Stitch them together and press the seams open. Finish the bottom edge of the facings.

13 With right sides together, matching the notches, pin the facings to the front and back bodices at the necklines. Stitch all around, taking care when sewing over the zip coil.

14 Snip into and trim the neckline seam allowance. Understitch (see page 40) the seam allowances to the facing.

15 Fold the back neck facing over to the right side of the back bodice, making sure that the centre back sections of the bodice and facing align. Pin the unstitched centre back edges of the facing to the zip seam allowance, catching the zip tape. Stitch the facing to the centre back seam allowance, as close as possible to the zip coil. Trim the top corner of the facing, turn the facing over to the wrong side of the bodice and press.

TOP TIP

On the right-hand bodice, trim the corner at the side edge to get a clean finish.

Sew the front skirts

16 Finish the waist edges of the front skirt pieces. With right sides together and waistline notches matching, pin the front skirt pieces to the corresponding bodice pieces at the waistline. You will notice that the right-hand skirt panel does not fully align with the bodice; this because the facing needs to be unfolded and pinned onto the skirt's waistline as well. The left-hand bodice does not have a vertical edge, so the left-hand front skirt will align at the waistline. Stitch the skirt and bodice sections together, then press the seams open.

17 With right sides together and notches matching, pin the front of the dress to the back at the side seam. Check that the waistline seams match, then sew the side edges together and press the seams open.

18 On the right-hand side of the bodice, fold the vertical edge of the facing to the wrong side. This will cause the front edge of the skirt to fold over as well. Press this new fold.

19 Finish the opening edge of the left skirt. Fold the opening edge to the wrong side by 1.5 cm (⅝ in.) and press. Topstitch as close to the finished edge as possible.

Hem the skirt

20 Finish the bottom edge of the skirt. Locate the diagonal edge at the hem of the right skirt. Pinch the diagonal edges right sides together and sew along that line. Trim the corner and press the seam open; the purpose of this is to reduce bulk at the corner.

21 Fold up the hem by 5.5 cm (about 2 in.) and press. Starting from the bottom edge of the left skirt, topstitch all around the bottom edge, then pivot and continue stitching up to the waistline of the right skirt.

22 To hold the inner portion of the wrap dress in place, fold over the left-hand side of the dress and pin the vertical edge to the seam allowance at the other side seam, matching the waist seams. Pin in place, then stitch down from the waistline for 5 cm (2 in.) along the seam allowance.

Sew the sleeves

23 To achieve a full effect at the sleeve hem, the sleeves have a lining piece with a narrower hem and width. Therefore, the sleeve hem needs to be eased in using gathering stitches. Sew two rows of gathering stitches (see page 39) along the bottom edge of the sleeves and pull the top threads to create gathers.

24 With right sides together and notches matching, lay the sleeve lining over the sleeve and pin them together at the bottom edge. Adjust the gathers until the sleeve hem matches the lining's hem, then stitch together.

25 Understitch (see page 40) the sleeve's seam allowance to the sleeve lining; this will ensure that the lining stays in place inside the sleeve.

26 Pull the lining down, away from the sleeve, then fold the sleeve in half. With right sides together, aligning the raw edges, pin and sew the sleeve and lining along the underarm edge. Press the seam open.

27 Pull the lining back into the sleeve and pin them together at the top edge. (Note that the lining is shorter than the sleeve.)

28 Sew gathering stitches around the sleeve head from notch to notch. Gently pull the top threads to form the gathers. Insert the sleeves into the armholes (see page 43). Adjust the gathers to ensure there are no puckers, then sew around the sleeve head through all layers. Finish the seam allowances and press the seams open.

Wrap Skirt

How much difference a carefully chosen finishing touch can make! The bold buckles on this skirt stand out against the plain wool-mix fabric and, with its neat waistband, this version looks altogether more tailored than the Wrap Dress. Made in a lightweight cotton with a wide waist tie instead of the buckles, it would make the perfect cover-up for sunny days on the beach.

Materials

- 1.8 m (2 yd) fabric, 150 cm (60 in.) wide
- 40 cm (16 in.) interfacing
- 4 x 4-cm (1½-in.) D-rings
- 23-cm (9-in.) zip
- Basic sewing kit (see page 32)

Difficulty level

Intermediate

Fabric suggestions

Washed wool, jacquard, cashmere crepe, needlecord

Design notes

Use a 1.5-cm (⅝-in.) seam allowance throughout, unless otherwise stated.

Finished garment measurements	8	10	12	14	16	18	20	22
Waist (cm)	67	72	77	82	87	92	97	102
Waist (in.)	26¼	28¼	30¼	32¼	34¼	36¼	38	40
Hip (cm)	97	102	107	112	117	122	127	132
Hip (in.)	38	40	42	44	46	48	50	52
Front length (cm)	68.5	69	69.5	70	71	71.5	72	72.5
Front length (in.)	27	27¼	27½	27½	28	28¼	28½	28½
Back length (cm)	69.5	70	70.5	71	72	72.5	73	73.5
Back length (in.)	27½	27½	27¾	28	28½	28½	28¾	29

CUTTING GUIDE

150 cm (60 in.) wide fabric

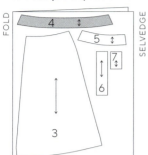
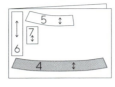

Interfacing

Single layer

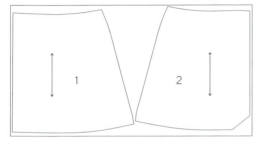

1 Left front skirt – cut 1

2 Right front skirt – cut 1

3 Back skirt – cut 1 pair

4 Front waist facing – cut 1 in fabric
and 1 in interfacing

5 Back waist facing – cut 1 pair in fabric
and 1 pair in interfacing

6 Belt – cut 1 pair in fabric and 1 pair in interfacing

7 Tab – cut 1 pair in fabric and 1 pair in interfacing

THE SEWING STARTS HERE

Prepare the pieces

1 Lay out the pattern pieces as shown in the cutting
guide. Cut out and transfer any markings to the
fabric (see page 37).

2 Following the manufacturer's instructions, apply
interfacing to the wrong side of the belt, tab and
front and back waist facings (see page 35).

Sew the belts and tabs

3 Fold the belt in half widthways, right sides
together. Sew along the long raw edge and one
short edge, leaving the other short end open.
Cut across the corner to create a crisp edge. Turn
right side out and press. Turn under the short raw
ends by 1 cm (⅜ in.) and press. Repeat with the
second belt. Sew the tabs in the same way.

4 Loop a stitched tab over the straight side of two
D-rings. Fold the tab in half and tack (baste)
across it to keep the rings in place. Repeat
with the other tab and D-rings.

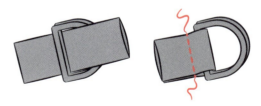

Assemble the skirt front

5 Finish the raw side edges of each skirt front piece.
Fold and press the opening edge of the left front
skirt to the wrong side by 1.5 cm (⅝ in.) and stitch
1.2 cm (½ in.) from the edge. Fold and press the
opening edge of the right front skirt to the wrong
side by 4 cm (1½ in.) and stitch 3.7cm (1⅜ in.) from
the folded edge.

6 Overlap the right (outer) front skirt over the left (inner) skirt, matching the centre front notches. Pin in place, then tack along the waistline to hold the skirts together.

7 Locate the tab markings on the right side of the left (inner) skirt. Pin, then topstitch the tabs and D-rings in place.

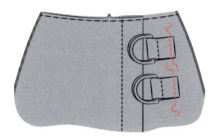

8 Locate the belt markings on the right side of the right (outer) skirt. With the belts pointing towards the side seam, pin and sew the belts in place, aligning the stitches with the stitches on the front opening edge of the skirt. Trim off the excess fabric.

9 Fold the belts away from the side seam and topstitch.

Sew the back skirt pieces

10 Pin and sew the darts on the back skirt pieces (see page 42). Press the darts towards the centre back.

11 Place the back pieces right sides together and pin along the centre back from the hem up to the zip notch. Stitch in place. Snip into the seam allowances at the zip notch, then press the seam allowances open.

12 Insert the zip in the centre back seam (see page 47). The zip end should sit 1 cm (⅜ in.) below the top edge to allow for the waist facing seam allowance. Topstitch the zip in place.

Assemble the skirt

13 Place the front and back pieces right sides together, then pin and stitch the side seams. Press the seams open.

14 Sew and attach the waist facings (see Special Technique: Waist Facing, page 145).

15 Finish the bottom edge of the skirt. Fold up the hem by 3 cm (1¼ in.) and press. Stitch all around the bottom edge.

VERSION 3

Jumpsuit

A wrap-over bodice and loose-fitting trouser section combine to create a relaxed style that will suit almost any figure – but what really makes this garment is the vibrant African wax print fabric, which simply pops with colour. This is a small-scale print; if you opt for something with a larger pattern repeat, take the time to pattern match.

Materials

- 3.2 m (3½ yd) fabric, 150 cm (60 in.) wide
- 50 cm (20 in.) interfacing
- 40-cm (16-in.) closed-end zip
- Basic sewing kit (see page 32)

Difficulty level

Intermediate

Fabric suggestions

Cotton, denim, chambray, linen, viscose, rayon, double gauze

Design notes

Use a 1.5-cm (⅝-in.) seam allowance throughout, unless otherwise stated.

CUTTING GUIDE

1 Waist tie –
cut 1 on fold

2 Front neck facing
– cut 1 pair in
fabric and 1 pair in
interfacing

3 Front trouser
– cut 1 pair

4 Sleeve – cut 1 pair

5 Bodice back
– cut 1 pair

6 Bodice front
– cut 1 pair

7 Waistband – cut 1 pair

8 Back neck facing
– cut 1 pair in
fabric and 1 pair
in interfacing

9 Back trouser
– cut 1 pair

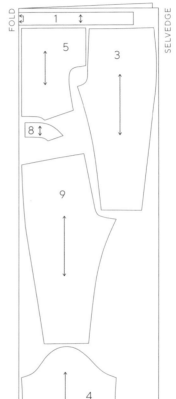

150 cm (60 in.) wide fabric

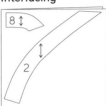

Interfacing

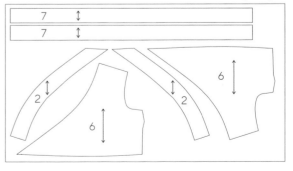

Single layer

Finished garment measurements	8	10	12	14	16	18	20	22
Bust (cm)	93	98	103	108	113	118	123	128
Bust (in.)	36½	38½	40½	42½	44½	46½	48½	50½
Front bodice length (cm)	43.5	44	44.5	45	46	46.5	47	47.5
Front bodice length (in.)	17	17¼	17½	17¾	18	18¼	18½	18¾
Back bodice length (cm)	41.5	42	42.5	43	44	44.5	45	45.5
Back bodice length (in.)	16¼	16½	16¾	17	17¼	17½	17¾	18
Waist (cm)	92	97	102	107	112	117	122	127
Waist (in.)	36	38	40	42	44	46	48	50
Hip (cm)	102.5	107.5	112.5	117.5	122.5	127.5	132.5	137.5
Hip (in.)	40½	42½	44¼	46¼	48¼	50¼	52¼	54
Sleeve length (cm)	30.5	31	31.5	32	32.5	33	33.5	34
Sleeve length (in.)	12	12¼	12½	12½	12¾	13	13¼	13½
Inside leg (cm)	64.5	64.5	64.5	64.5	64.5	64.5	64.5	64.5
Inside leg (in.)	25½	25½	25½	25½	25½	25½	25½	25½

THE SEWING STARTS HERE

Prepare the pieces

1 Lay out the pattern pieces as shown in the cutting guide. Cut out and transfer any markings to the fabric (see page 37).

2 Following the manufacturer's instruction, apply interfacing to the wrong side of the front and back neck facings (see page 35).

3 Stay stitch (see page 40) the necklines of the front and back bodice sections.

Construct the wrap bodice

4 Mark and stitch the front bodice bust darts (see page 42). Press the darts downwards.

5 Finish the centre back bodice edges and insert the zip (see page 47). With right sides together, sew the centre back seam below the zip. Press the seam open.

6 With right sides together, pin and sew the front and back bodices together at the shoulders. Finish the seam allowances. Press the seams open.

7 With right sides together, pin and sew the front and back facings together at the shoulders. Press the seams open. Finish the bottom and centre back edges.

8 With right sides together, matching the notches, pin the facing around the bodice neckline. You will find that there is more fabric around the bodice neckline than there is around the facing, so gently ease the fabric as you go; this will ensure that the neckline lies flat. Fold the centre back edges of the facing to the wrong side by 1.5 cm (⅝ in.) and press. These edges will be stitched to the zip tape later.

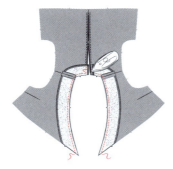

9 With the facing uppermost, working from the bottom of the front bodice to the centre back on each side, stitch the facing in place, taking care not to stitch the centre back edges of the facing that you folded back in step 8; the feed dogs on your machine will help to ease the excess fabric through. Trim the seam allowances and snip into the curves. Understitch (see page 40) the facing to the seam allowances. Turn the facing to the wrong side of the garment and press.

10 Pin the folded edge at the centre back of the facing to the zip tape. With the right side of the garment facing up, stitch 'in the ditch' (see page 40) along the original zip stitching to secure the facing in place.

11 Press the neckline and overlap the front bodice pieces. Making sure that the centre front notches match, pin them together at the waistline Check the fit around your waistline and make any adjustments before tacking (basting) the overlapped edges together.

12 Fold the bodice in half, with right sides together, matching the underarm and side edges. Pin and sew the underarm and side seam on each side. Finish the seam allowances and press the seams open.

Construct the sleeves

13 Pin the underarm edges of each sleeve right sides together and sew from one end to the other. Finish the seam allowances and press the seams open.

14 At the sleeve ends, fold 1 cm (⅜ in.) to the wrong side, followed by a further 1.5 cm (⅝ in.) and press. Sew close to the fold.

15 Around each sleeve head, sew two lines of gathering stitches (see page 39) between the notches. Gently pull the top threads to gather the stitches.

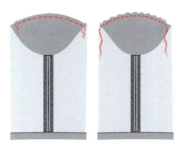

16 With right sides together and front and back notches matching, pin the sleeves in place. Distribute the gathers evenly so that the sleeves fit into the armholes. Stitch the sleeves in place and finish the seam allowances together (see page 38).

Construct the trousers

17 With right sides together, matching the notches, pin each trouser front to the matching trouser back. Sew along the side edges and inseams. Finish the seam allowances and press the seams open.

18 Turn one trouser leg right side out and insert it into the other trouser leg, matching the inseams and notches. Pin and sew them together around the crotch. Finish the seam allowances and press the seam open. Turn the trousers right side out.

Create the waistband

19 On one waistband piece, pin and sew the short edges right sides together and press the seam open. Fold the bottom edge of this piece to the wrong side by 1.5 cm (⅝ in.) and press. This will be the inner waistband.

20 The other piece will be the outer waistband. Pin the short edges wrong sides together, mark the seam allowance 1.5 cm (⅝ in.) from the raw edges, then draw another vertical line 2 cm (¾ in.) long in the middle of the seam allowance line; this section will be left open for the ties.

Starting at the top of the waistband, sew down the seam allowance as far as the top of the waist tie line, then backstitch and cut the threads. Sew from the other end of the waist tie line to the bottom of the waistband, then backstitch and cut the threads.

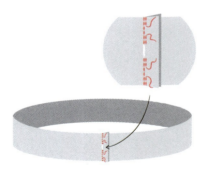

21 Fold in the seam allowances by 6 mm (¼ in.) and press. Then press open the remaining wseam allowance. To reinforce the hole, topstitch around it to form a narrow rectangle.

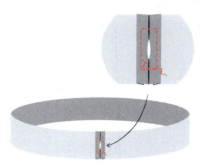

Join the bodice and trouser sections

22 Locate the notches on both waistband pieces and pin them to the bodice waistband. The outer waistband and bodice should be right sides together; the right side of the inner waistband should be against the wrong side of the bodice. The vertical hole should be positioned at the centre front.

23 Stitch around the waistline through all the fabric layers, then understitch (see page 40) the seam allowances to the inner waistband to help the waistband lie flat. Press the waistbands and seam allowances downwards.

24 Move the inner waistband out of the way. With right sides together, matching the notches, pin the waistline of the trousers to the bottom edge of the outer waistband. The centre front seam of the waistband should match the centre front seam of the trousers. Sew around the waistline, making sure you don't catch the inner waistband in the stitching. Press the seam allowances upwards.

25 Pin the folded edge of the inner waistband to the waistband of the trousers, making sure it covers the waist seam allowances. Using a hand sewing needle and matching thread, slipstitch the inner waistband to the seam allowances.

26 Fold the tie in half lengthways, right sides together, and sew along the unfolded long edge, then turn the tie right side out. Tuck in 1.5 cm (⅝ in.) at each short end and topstitch the openings. Press the waist tie and carefully insert it into the waistband channel using a bodkin or safety pin.

Hem the trousers

27 Finish the raw edges of the trouser legs. Fold 2.5 cm (1 in.) to the wrong side and press. Sew around the hem close to the fold.

Shirred Garments

Shirring imitates the much more time-consuming smocking technique that was traditionally used on baby clothes – but as you can see here, you can apply it to everything from country-style dresses to chic tops for evening wear.

Shirred Dress

This traditional 'peasant-style' dress, with shirring on the bodice and cuffs, is perfect for summer. The choice of a crisp, brightly coloured gingham fabric adds to the country feel.

Materials

- 3.4 m (3¾ yd) fabric, 150 cm (60 in.) wide
- 3 reels shirring elastic
- 2 m (2¼ yd) elastic, 1 cm (⅜ in.) wide
- Basic sewing kit (see page 32)

Difficulty level

Intermediate

Fabric suggestions

Double gauze, cotton poplin, viscose, crepe de chine, silk, African wax fabric, linen

Design notes

Use a 1.5-cm (⅝-in.) seam allowance throughout, unless otherwise stated.

Finished garment measurements

	8	10	12	14	16	18	20	22
Length (cm)	109.5	110	110.5	111	112	112.5	113	113.5
Length (in.)	43	43¼	43½	43¾	44	44¼	44½	44¾
Bust (cm)	75	80	85	90	95	100	105	110
Bust (in.)	29½	31½	33½	35½	37½	39½	41½	43¼
Waist (cm)	75	80	85	90	95	100	105	110
Waist (in.)	29½	31½	33½	35½	37½	39½	41½	43¼
Hip (cm)	185	190	195	200	205	210	215	220
Hip (in.)	73	74¾	76¾	78¾	80¾	82¾	82¾	86½
Sleeve length (cm)	56.5	57	57.5	58	58.5	59	59.5	60
Sleeve length (in.)	22¼	22½	22¾	22¾	23	23¼	23½	23¾

CUTTING GUIDE

150 cm (60 in.) wide fabric

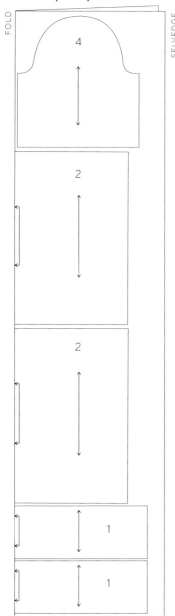

1 Shirring panel – cut 2 on the fold

2 Skirt – cut 2 on the fold

3 Bodice – cut 2 in shirred fabric

4 Sleeve – cut 1 pair

THE SEWING STARTS HERE

Prepare the pieces

1 Lay out the pattern pieces as shown in the cutting guide. Note that the front and back bodice pieces will be cut once the shirring has been done, so do not cut these just yet. Cut out all the other pieces and transfer any markings to the fabric (see page 37).

2 Sew the shirring lines on the shirring panels (see Special Technique: Shirring, page 93). There are 15 lines of shirring on each one and the bodice pieces will be cut from these.

Construct the bodice

3 Place the front and back bodice patterns on the shirring panels, pin in place and carefully cut them out.

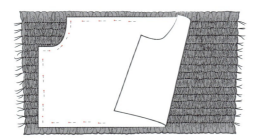

4 Re-thread your bobbin with normal sewing thread. Finish the raw edges of the shirred front and back bodice pieces along the top, bottom and armhole edges; you can either overlock (serge) them or use zigzag stitch..

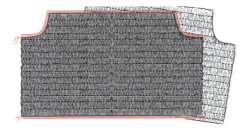

5 Along the top edge of the front and back bodice pieces, fold 1.5 cm (⅝ in.) to the wrong side. Pin in place, then stitch 1.2 cm (½ in.) from the fold to create a channel.

6 Thread a 27-cm (10½-in.) length of 1-cm (⅜-in.) wide elastic through each channel. Machine tack (baste) across each end to hold the elastic in place.

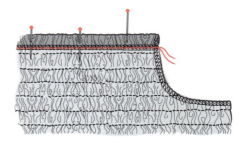

7 With right sides together, pin and stitch the shirred bodice pieces together along the side seams. Finish the seam allowances.

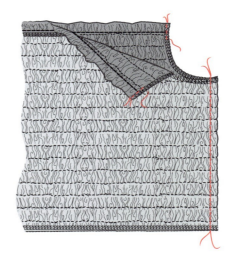

Sew the skirt

8 Finish the raw top and side edges of the front and back skirt panels.

9 With right sides together, pin and stitch the front and back skirt panels together along the side seams.

10 Sew gathering stitches (see page 39) along the top edge of the skirt. Pull the gathers to match the length of the bottom edge of the bodice, making sure the gathers are distributed evenly.

Attach the bodice to the skirt

11 With right sides together, matching the sides seams of bodice and skirt, pin the lower edge of the bodice around the gathered waist edge. Stitch around the waistline using a 1.5-cm (⅝-in.) seam allowance.

12 Press the seam allowance down towards the skirt.

13 Cut a 76-cm (30-in.) length of 1-cm (⅜-in.) wide elastic. Overlap the ends by 1 cm (⅜ in.) and stitch them together to form a loop.

14 Place the elastic under the waist seam allowance and pin the edge of the seam allowance down. Stitch the edge of the seam allowance down all the way around to create a channel containing the elastic, taking care not to catch the elastic in the stitching.

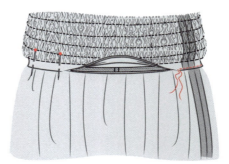

Sew the hem

15 At the hem of the skirt, turn 1 cm (⅜ in.) and then a further 1 cm (⅜ in.) to the wrong side and press. Sew in place.

SPECIAL TECHNIQUE: SHIRRING

Shirring is a really easy technique that gives a lovely smocked effect on fabric. It's important to make up the shirred panel before you assemble your garment, so that you can make sure it's the exact size you need. Mark your shirring lines really carefully before you start. You need a sewing machine, elastic sewing thread for the bobbin and regular thread for the needle.

1   Wind your bobbin with the elastic thread by hand: aim for a little bit of tension when you do this, without fully using the elasticity of the thread. Distribute the thread evenly around the bobbin, and set up the rest of your machine as usual.

2   Lower the needle tension on your machine and do a sample stitch: you should see the elastic bobbin thread on the back and only the needle thread on the front.

3   Start your first line, and don't backstitch. After a few stitches, tie up the needle and bobbin threads by hand at the start of your line. When you reach the end of your first line, tie the thread ends by hand again instead of backstitching.

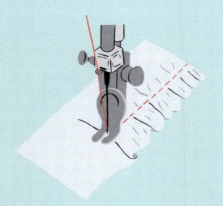

4   Sew all subsequent rows by pulling the fabric flat, to achieve even lines.

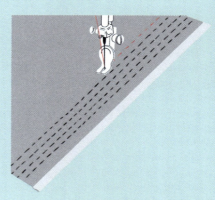

TIPS

○ **If your stitches are not gathering and the elastic looks loose on the back: change your bobbin tension.**

○ **If the needle thread looks as if it's only looping around the elastic on the back: change your needle tension.**

○ **If you are sewing lots of rows, check your bobbin thread regularly, as the elastic thread will run out much quicker than you think! You won't be able to restart halfway through a line of stitching once the bobbin thread has run out.**

○ **When you finish sewing each row, be sure to pull the elastic thread a long way out. If you cut it too close to the fabric, it may ping back inside the bobbin and unthread.**

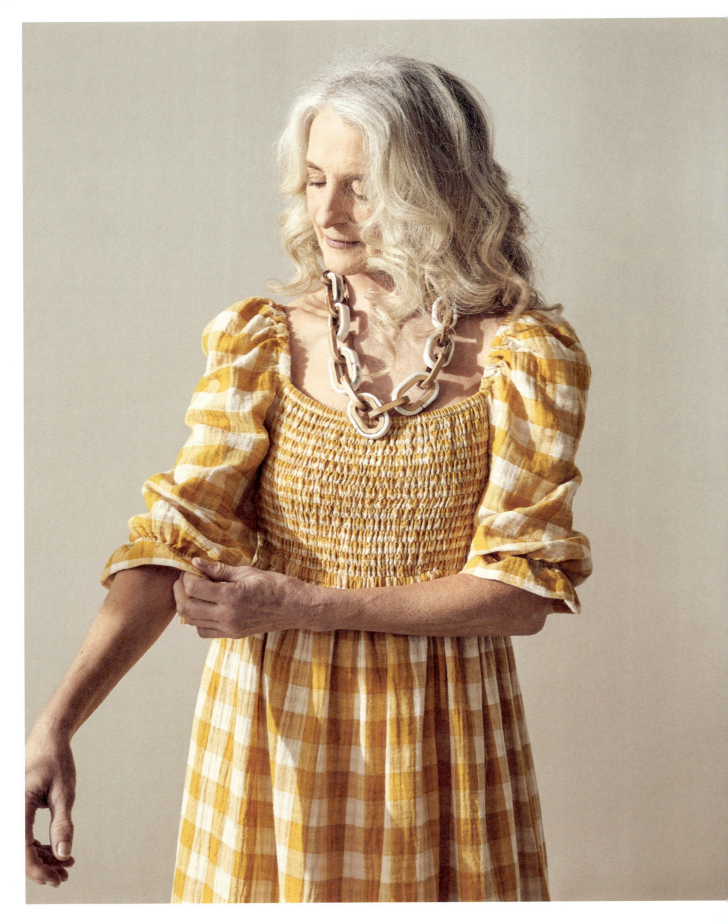

Sew the sleeves

16 Overlock the edges of the sleeves all the way around.

17 At the hem edge of the sleeves, turn 6 cm (2½ in.) to the wrong side and press. Machine tack to hold in place.

18 Following the pattern markings, sew three lines of shirring stitches on each sleeve (see Special Technique: Shirring, page 93), catching the hem edge of the sleeve in the first row.

19 Press 1.5 cm (⅝ in.) to the wrong side around the sleeve heads, pin in place, then sew between the notches to create a channel. Cut two 27-cm (10 ½-in.) lengths of 1-cm (⅜-in.) wide elastic and thread one through each channel, so that it extends 1 cm (⅜ in.) beyond the notch. Stitch across both end of the elastic to secure it in place.

20 Fold the sleeves in half lengthways, right sides together. Pin, then stitch the underarm seams. Press the seams open.

21 Pin the sleeves around the bottom of the armholes, from the bottom edge of the elastic to the other end of the elastic, then stitch in place (see page 43). Press the seams towards the sleeves.

22 Press the dress carefully.

Scrunchie

This easy-to-sew scunchie is made in the same fabric as the colourful country-style dress, but obviously the sky's the limit here! Use it as a wrist ornament or to keep your hair tied back.

Materials

- 50 x 10 cm (20 x 4 in.) of your chosen fabric
- 22 cm (8½ in.) elastic, 1 cm (⅜ in.) wide
- Basic sewing kit (see page 32)
- Turning tool

Difficulty level

Beginner

Fabric suggestions

Leftovers from woven fabrics like satin, cotton, viscose, silk, crepe

Design notes

Use a 1.5-cm (⅝-in.) seam allowance throughout, unless otherwise stated.

THE SEWING STARTS HERE

1   At one short end of your fabric rectangle, press 1 cm (⅜ in.) to the wrong side. With right sides together, fold the fabric in half lengthways and pin. Stitch along the long raw edge to form a tube with both short ends open. Press the seam open.

2   Turn the tube right side out and position the seam in the middle of one side.

3   Attach a safety pin to one end of the elastic, then feed it through the tube. Zigzag stitch the two ends of the elastic together to form a loop.

4   Carefully tuck the raw end of the tube inside the tube and pin in place. Either slipstitch the fabric in place by hand or stitch across the opening on your machine; note that if you machine stitch, the elastic will be sewn down.

Shirred Strappy Dress

Here, the shirring is limited to two relatively narrow panels, with the bulk of the bodice sitting in between; the shirring pulls the bodice panel in, creating an informal 'blousy' effect. The lightweight crepe fabric drapes beautifully and the monochrome colour scheme instantly gives a more modern feel.

Materials

- 2.4 m (2¾ yd) fabric, 150 cm (60 in.) wide
- 2 reels shirring elastic
- Basic sewing kit (see page 32)
- Rolled hem foot (optional)
- Turning tool

Difficulty level

Intermediate

Fabric suggestions

Double gauze, cotton poplin, viscose, crepe de chine, silk

Design notes

Use a 1.5-cm (⅝-in.) seam allowance throughout, unless otherwise stated.

Finished garment measurements	8	10	12	14	16	18	20	22
Front length (cm)	97.5	97.5	97.5	97.5	97.5	97.5	97.5	97.5
Front length (in.)	38½	38½	38½	38½	38½	38½	38½	38½
Back length (cm)	91.5	91.5	91.5	91.5	91.5	91.5	91.5	91.5
Back length (in.)	36	36	36	36	36	36	36	36
Bust (cm)	116.5	121.5	126.5	131.5	136.5	141.5	146.5	151.5
Bust (in.)	45¾	47¾	49¾	51¾	53¾	55¾	57¾	59¾
Waist (cm)	116.5	121.5	126.5	131.5	136.5	141.5	146.5	151.5
Waist (in.)	45¾	47¾	49¾	51¾	53¾	55¾	57¾	59¾
Hip (cm)	123	128	133	138	143	148	153	158
Hip (in.)	48½	50½	52½	54¼	56¼	58¼	60¼	62¼

CUTTING GUIDE

1 Back bodice top panel – cut 1 on the fold

2 Back bodice mid panel – cut 1 on the fold

3 Back waist panel – cut 1 on the fold

4 Back skirt – cut 1 on the fold

5 Front bodice top panel – cut 1 on the fold

6 Front bodice mid panel – cut 1 on the fold

7 Front waist panel – cut 1 on the fold

8 Front skirt – cut 1 on the fold

9 Shoulder strap – cut 1 pair

150 cm (60 in.) wide fabric

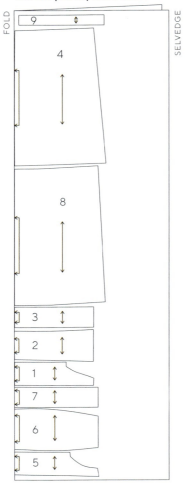

THE SEWING STARTS HERE

Prepare the pieces

1 Lay out the pattern pieces as shown in the cutting guide. Cut out and transfer any markings to the fabric (see page 37).

2 Finish the top, bottom and armhole edges of the front and back bodice top panels (see page 38).

3 At the top edge of both front and back bodice top panel pieces, fold 6 mm (¼ in.) to the wrong side and stitch it down to create a narrow hem. Alternatively, use a rolled hem foot to create a narrow rolled hem (see page 42).

4 Sew the shirring lines on the front and back top bodice and waist panels (see Special Technique: Shirring, page 93). There should be six lines of shirring 8 mm (⁵⁄₁₆ in.) apart on each piece. You can either mark the shirring lines on the fabric or stitch them freehand.

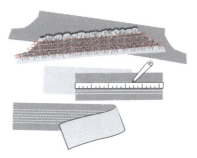

Sew the bodice

5 With right sides together, pin the shirred bodice top panel pieces to the top edge of the mid panels. With the shirring elastic still on the bobbin, sew the panels together. Press the seam allowances down towards the waistline. (The shirring elastic will be on the top panels' side of the seam and the regular thread on the mid panels' side of the seam.) Repeat on the back panels.

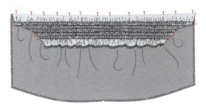

TOP TIP

You will have to stretch the shirred panels to get them to fit the mid panels; when stitched, the mid panels will gather up.

6 With right sides together, pin the top edge of the shirred waist panels to the bottom edge of the mid panels. With the shirring elastic still on the bobbin, sew the panels together. (The shirring elastic will be on the shirred waist panels' side.) Press the seam allowances down towards the waistline. Repeat on the back panels.

7 Measure the circumference of the armhole, add 2 cm (¾ in.) and cut two strips of fabric on the bias to this length by 2 cm (¾ in.) wide. Fold the strip in half lengthways and press. Open the strip out, then fold the long edges in to the centre and press again.

8 Re-thread your bobbin with normal sewing thread. Bind the armholes, using the concealed method (see page 183) and snipping into the curves before turning the binding over to the wrong side for a neat finish.

9 Place the two bodice pieces right sides together, then pin and stitch the side seams. Finish the raw edges.

Sew the straps

10 Fold the straps in half lengthways, right sides together, and sew along the long raw edge. Use a turning tool to turn the straps right side out. Turn in the raw edges at each end by 1 cm (⅜ in.). Press.

11 Matching the folded edges of the straps and the markings at the top edge of the dress, pin the straps in place on the wrong side of the bodice. Topstitch the straps in place by sewing over the shirring stitches at the top edge.

Sew the skirt

12 Finish the waist and side edges of the front and back skirts. With right sides together, pin and stitch the front and back skirt panels together along the side seams. Press the seams open.

Attach the skirt to the bodice

13 Thread your bobbin with shirring elastic. With right sides together, matching the side seams of the bodice and skirt, pin the lower edge of the bodice around the top edge of the waist. Stitch around the waistline. (The shirring elastic will be on the shirred waist panels' side.) Press the seam down towards the skirt.

Sew the hem

14 Around the bottom of the skirt, turn 1 cm (⅜ in.) and then a further 1 cm (⅜ in.) to the wrong side and press. Sew in place. Press the dress.

Shirred Top

The sheer fabric, high collar and long raglan sleeves give this garment a more sophisticated look that is great for evening wear. Unusually, the shirring is done on the collar, cuffs and waist panel, rather than on the bodice, creating stylish detailing.

Materials

- Sizes 8–14: 1.7 m (1⅞ yd) fabric, 150 cm (60 in.) wide
  Sizes 16–22: 2 m (2¼ yd) fabric, 150 cm (60 in.) wide

- 1 reel shirring elastic

- 20 cm (8 in.) of 3-mm (⅛-in.) round elastic cord

- 4 buttons, 1 cm (⅜ in.) in diameter

- Basic sewing kit (see page 32)

- Rolled hem foot (optional)

Difficulty level

Advanced

Fabric suggestions

Silk organza, georgette, tulle, chiffon

Design notes

Use a 1.5-cm (⅝-in.) seam allowance throughout, unless otherwise stated.

Finished garment measurements	8	10	12	14	16	18	20	22
Front length (cm)	66.5	67	67.5	68	69	69.5	70	70.5
Front length (in.)	26	26¼	26½	26¾	27	27¼	27½	27¾
Back length (cm)	62.5	63	63.5	64	65	65.5	66	66.5
Back length (in.)	24½	24¾	25	25¼	25½	25¾	26	26¼
Bust (cm)	97	102	107	112	117	122	127	132
Bust (in.)	38	40	42	44	46	48	50	52
Sleeve length (cm)	71.5	72	73	74	74.5	75.5	76	77
Sleeve length (in.)	28	28½	28¾	29	29¼	29¾	30	30¼
Waist (cm)	97.5	102.5	107.5	112.5	117.5	122.5	127.5	132.5
Waist (in.)	38¼	40¼	42¼	44¼	46¼	48¼	50¼	52¼

CUTTING GUIDE

1 Front bodice – cut 1 on the fold

2 Back bodice – cut 1 pair

3 Sleeve – cut 1 pair

4 Cuff – cut 1 pair

5 Collar – cut 1

6 Front bodice bottom panel – cut 1 on the fold

7 Back bodice bottom panel – cut 1 on the fold

8 Front waistband – cut 1 on the fold

9 Back waistband – cut 1 on the fold

THE SEWING STARTS HERE

Prepare the pieces

1 Lay out the pattern pieces as shown in the cutting guide. Cut out and transfer any markings to the fabric (see page 37). Cut a strip of fabric on the bias measuring 7 cm x 32 mm (3 x 1¼ in.) to conceal the button loops.

2 Finish (see page 38) the armholes on the front and back bodices and the sleeves.

Sizes 8–14: 150 cm (60 in.) wide fabric

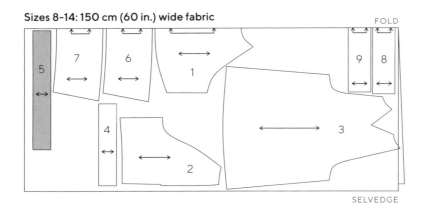

Sizes 16–22: 150 cm (60 in.) wide fabric

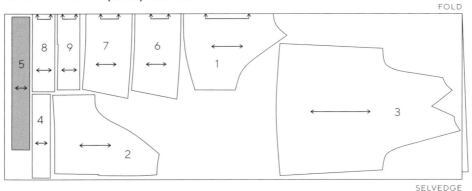

Construct the sleeves

3 Locate the dart markings at the sleeve heads and mark the dart point. Finish the raw edge of the dart opening, then pin and stitch the darts (see page 42) and press them open.

Assemble the bodice

4 With right sides together and notches matching, pin and stitch the sleeves to the front and back bodice pieces. Finish the seam allowances and press the seams open.

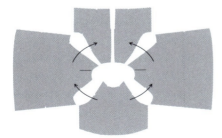

Shir the collar and cuff

5 Sew a narrow rolled hem (see page 42) on one long edge of the collar and cuffs.

6 Referring to the pattern for the placement, work four lines of shirring on the collar and cuffs and six lines of shirring (see Special Technique: Shirring, page 93) on each of the two waistband panels. The lines should be 8 mm (⁵⁄₁₆ in.) apart. You can either mark the shirring lines on the fabric or stitch them freehand. Note: each shirring line should stop within the seam allowances, just 1 cm (³⁄₈ in.) shy of the edge of the fabric pieces.

Attach the collar and cuffs

7 With right sides together and the edges of the collar matching the centre back edges of the bodice, pin the unhemmed long edge of the collar to the neckline. With the shirring elastic still on the bobbin, sew the collar in place. (The shirring elastic will be on the collar side of the seam and the regular thread on the bodice side.) Finish the seam allowances. Press the collar and seam allowances upwards.

8 Gather (see page 39) the bottom edge of the sleeves to approx. 35 cm (13¾ in.).

9 With the shirring elastic still on the bobbin, pin the unhemmed long edge of the cuffs to the sleeves, adjusting the gathers to fit if necessary. Sew in place. (The shirring elastic will be on the sleeve side of the seam and the regular thread on the cuff's side.) Finish the seam allowances.

Sew the side and centre back seams

10 Re-thread your bobbin with normal sewing thread. Place the front and back bodices right sides together, matching the sleeve underarms and the side seams. Pin and stitch from the hem to the sleeve cuffs in one continuous line on each side. Finish the seam allowances together and press the seams to one side.

11 At the centre back, finish the raw edges from collar to waistline. Then locate the notches on the centre back. Pin the centre back pieces right sides together and sew from the notches to the waistline. Press the seam open.

12 Fold the unstitched section of the back bodice to the wrong side by 1.5 cm (⅝ in.) and press in place.

Create the button loops

13 Cut four 5-cm (2-in.) lengths of round elastic cord. Fold each one in half to form a loop. Following the markings on the pattern, pin them to the right-hand side of the collar (as worn), on the wrong side of the garment, and tack (baste) in place.

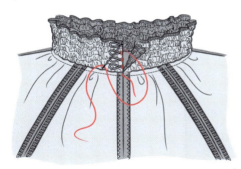

14 Take the bias strip you cut in step 1 and fold both short ends to the wrong side by 1 cm (⅜ in.). Fold both long edges to the wrong side by 6 mm (¼ in.) and press. Open out one long edge. Align it with the cut ends of the elastic cords, right side down, and sew along the crease line. Fold over the bias strip to the right side of the garment and topstitch as close as possible to the folded edge to completely conceal the ends of the elastic.

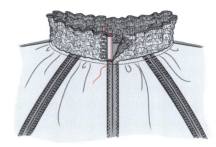

15 Turn the bodice right side out. Starting at the top of the collar, sew down the pressed seam allowance at the centre back opening, pivoting at the corners, and up the other side of the opening (the side for the buttons).

Attach the waistband

16 Pin and sew the short ends of the two shirred waistband pieces right sides together. Finish the seam allowances together and press the seams to one side. Repeat with the bodice bottom panels.

17 Re-thread your bobbin with shirring elastic. With right sides together, pin and sew the top edge of the shirred waistband to the bottom edge of the bodice. Then pin and sew the other edge of the waistband to the bodice bottom panel in the same way. (Sew with the bodice panels uppermost, so that the shirring elastic will be on the waistband's side of the seam.) Finish the seam allowances and press towards the hem.

18 Re-thread your bobbin with regular sewing thread. Fold the hem to the wrong side by 6 mm (¼ in.), press and stitch. Alternatively, stitch a narrow rolled hem. Lightly press the top.

19 Mark the locations of the four buttons in the middle of the loops. Using a matching thread, hand stitch the buttons to the outside of the collar, on the left-hand side as worn.

Sheer and Semi-sheer Fabrics

Sheer and semi-sheer fabrics require careful handling and sewing, so they are not projects for complete beginners. In this section you'll find ideas for layering them together and using frills to add volume and create a fun decorative feature.

1960s Dance Dress

Made in a slippery crepe backed satin and tulle fabric, this dress requires careful handling and some precise sewing so it is not a project for beginners. The scoop-necked bodice consists of two layers that are 'bagged out' for a really neat finish at the neckline and armholes. The circle skirt creates a lovely sense of movements and features two layers – an opaque underskirt topped by a transparent overskirt.

Materials

- 2 m (2¼ yd) fabric, 150 cm (60 in.) wide
- 1.5 m (1⅝ yd) sheer fabric, 150 cm (60 in.) wide
- 30 cm (12 in.) interfacing
- 56-cm (22-in.) zip
- Basic sewing kit (see page 32)

Difficulty level

Confident sewer

Fabric suggestions

Underskirt and bodice: Satin-backed crepe fabric, taffeta, duchesse satin

Sheer overskirt: Drapey and lightweight fabrics like georgette, voile, tulle, silk organza, lace

Design notes

Use a 1.5-cm (⅝-in.) seam allowance throughout, unless otherwise stated.

Note that the bodice consists of two layers that are 'bagged out', so you need to cut a pair of each pattern piece. We used the same fabric for both the outer layer and the lining, but you could use a different fabric for the lining if you prefer.

Finished garment measurements	8	10	12	14	16	18	20	22
Bust (cm)	79	84	89	94	99	104	109	114
Bust (in.)	31	33	35	37	39	41	43	45
Waist (cm)	63	68	73	78	83	88	93	98
Waist (in.)	24¾	26¾	28¾	30¾	32¾	34¾	36½	38½
Front length (cm)	92.5	93	93.5	94	95	95.5	96	96.5
Front length (in.)	36½	36½	36¾	37	37½	37½	37¾	38
Back length, nape to hem (cm)	69	69.5	70	70.5	71.5	72	72.5	73
Back length, nape to hem (in.)	27	27¼	27½	27¾	28	28¼	28½	28¾

CUTTING GUIDE

150 cm (60 in.) wide fabric

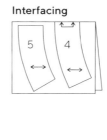

FOLD

1

1

4

7

6

5

2

3

3

5

2

SELVEDGE

Sheer FOLD

7

6

SELVEDGE

Interfacing

5

4

1. Front bodice – cut 1 on the fold in main fabric and 1 on the fold in lining fabric

2. Side bodice – cut 1 pair in main fabric and 1 pair in lining fabric

3. Back bodice – cut 1 pair in main fabric and 1 pair in lining fabric

4. Front waistband – cut 1 on the fold in main fabric and 1 on the fold in interfacing

5. Back waistband – cut 2 pairs in main fabric and 1 pair in interfacing

6. Front skirt – cut 1 on the fold in main fabric and 1 on the fold in sheer fabric

7. Back skirt – cut 1 pair in main fabric and 1 pair in sheer fabric

THE SEWING STARTS HERE

Prepare the pieces

1 Lay out the pattern pieces as shown in the cutting guide. Cut out and transfer any markings to the fabric (see page 37).

2 Following the manufacturer's instructions, apply interfacing to the wrong side of one front waistband piece and one pair of back waistband pieces (see page 35).

Sew the bodice

3 Pin and sew the waist darts in the front bodice (see page 42). Press the darts towards the side seams. Repeat with the second front bodice.

4 With right sides together, aligning the bottom and side raw edges, pin and sew a side bodice piece to each back bodice piece. Press the seams open. You will now have four back pieces, each consisting of a back and a side piece joined together.

5 With right sides together, pin and stitch a combined back-and-side piece to each side of your two front bodice pieces. Press the seams open.

6 Place the two bodices right sides together. Pin and stitch around the curved neck sections, then snip into the curves (see page 39).

7 Press one bodice and the seam allowances up around the neck edges. This will be your bodice lining. Understitch (see page 40) the neck edge, stitching 2mm (1/16 in.) away from the edge on the bodice lining and finishing 1.5 cm (5/8 in.) from the centre back edge on each side.

8 Bring the two bodices right sides together again and pin and stitch the armholes. Snip into the curves.

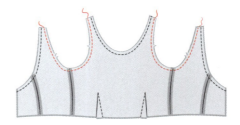

9 Turn the bodice right side out and press the neck and armhole seams.

10 With right sides together and shoulders matching, pin the shoulder seams. On the front bodice, unpick the first and last 1.5 cm (⅝ in.) of stitching at the neck and armholes. Pin the back pieces to just the front bodice and move the front lining edge out of the way. Stitch across the three layers of shoulder seams. Press the seam allowance towards the front bodice.

11 Fold in the seam allowance at the shoulders of the front bodice lining. Pin and hand stitch it in place over the seam allowances of the back bodice lining, stitching through the two lining layers only. Where you unpicked part of the neck and armhole edges in the previous step, slipstitch the two layers of the front bodice together.

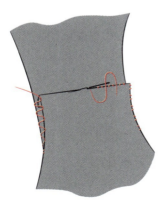

Prepare the waistband pieces

12 With right sides together, pin the **interfaced back waistband** pieces to the **interfaced front waistband** at the side seams. Stitch, then press the seams towards to the centre back. Repeat with the **non-interfaced waistband pieces**.

Assemble the main fabric skirt

13 On your main fabric skirt pieces, overlock (serge) the side and centre back edges. With right sides together, pin the back skirt pieces to the front skirt and stitch the side seams. Press the seams open.

14 Pin the centre back pieces together and stitch from the hem up to the notch at the bottom of the zip. Press the seam open.

Assemble the sheer fabric skirt

15 The side seams of the sheer skirt layer are stitched using a French seam, which encloses the raw edges of the seam allowances. With **wrong** sides together, pin the sheer back skirt pieces to the sheer front skirt and sew, taking a 5-mm (³⁄₁₆-in.) seam allowance. Trim the seam allowance carefully.

16 Press the back pieces over the seam allowances and fold so that the pieces are right sides together, with the previous seams right on the fold. Pin in place and stitch, again taking a 5-mm (³⁄₁₆-in.) seam allowance. Press the seams towards the centre back.

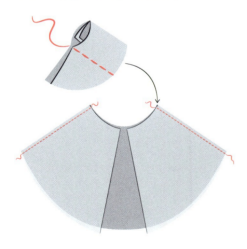

17 On the centre back edges, overlock the edges separately. With right sides together, stitch the seam from the hem to the zip notch. Snip into the seam allowance at the zip notch.

Attach the skirt to the waistband

18 With both skirts right side out, slide the sheer skirt over the main fabric skirt and tack (baste) around the top edge. With right sides together, matching the seams, pin the **interfaced waistband** around the top edge of the two skirt layers. Then pin the right side of the **non-interfaced waistband** to the wrong side of the skirt, so that the two skirt layers are sandwiched in between the two waistbands. Stitch together, clip the curve, then press the waistbands upwards.

1. INTERFACED WAISTBAND
2. SHEER SKIRT
3. MAIN FABRIC SKIRT
4. NON-INTERFACED WAISTBAND

TOP TIP

You will have to clip the top edge of the skirt slightly to fit the waistband.

19 On the **non-interfaced waistband**, turn the seam allowance to the wrong side and press.

Attach the bodice to the skirt

20 With right sides together, pin the bodice to the **interfaced waistband** and stitch in place. Do not attach the non-interfaced waistband – hold or pin it out of the way while you stitch. Press the seam down, towards the hem.

21 Bring the **non-interfaced waistband** up and pin it in place from the right side of the dress. Stitch 'in the ditch' (see page 40) around the bodice and waistband.

Insert the zip

22 At the centre back, machine tack all the layers together. Along the zip opening, press the seam allowances of the bodice and skirt to the wrong side. Insert the zip, using the lapped zip method (see Special Technique: Lapped Zip, opposite).

Sew the hem

23 On the main fabric skirt layer, overlock the hem edge, then press up 1 cm (⅜ in.) all the way around. Pin in place, then stitch 8 mm (⁵⁄₁₆ in.) from the edge.

24 Check that the sheer fabric skirt layer hasn't dropped before you stitch the hem. Trim off 6 mm (¼ in.) of the hem allowance on the sheer layer, then roll hem it either by hand or by machine using a rolled hem foot (see page 42).

SPECIAL TECHNIQUE: LAPPED ZIP

A lapped zip has one edge of fabric lapping the other, so that only one row of stitching is visible; the other edge is stitched very close to the zip teeth. Lapped zips are often used in side seams and in centre back seams.

1 Stitch the seam from the bottom of the zip to the garment's hemline. Press the seam open and press the seam allowance open on either side of the zip opening.

2 Working from the right side of the garment, pin the zip tape to the left-hand seam allowance, aligning the raw edges of the top of the zip tapes with the raw edge of the garment. Tack (baste) 6 mm (¼ in.) away from the teeth. Fit a regular zip foot and, with the zip open, topstitch this side of the zip, working from the bottom upwards.

3 Close the zip and lap the unjoined side of the garment over the topstitching. Pin in place. Tack as close as you can to the teeth.

4 Using a zip foot, stitch across the bottom of the zip tapes. Leave the needle down and turn the piece so you can stitch up to the top of the zip. Remove the tacking and press with a hot iron to settle the stitches.

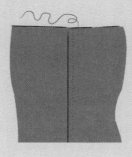

Midi Dance Skirt

This skirt is made in a lightweight sheer organza fabric that drapes well and has a lovely sheen. A frill at the hemline extends the length – a handy tip if you've accidentally cut your fabric too short! – and also adds volume.

150 cm (60 in.) wide fabric

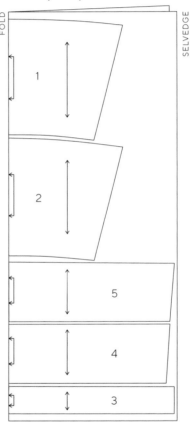

Materials

- 2 m (2¼ yd) fabric, 150 cm (60 in.) wide
- 2 m (2¼ yd) elastic, 4 cm (1½ in.) wide
- Basic sewing kit (see page 32)

Difficulty level

Beginner

Fabric suggestions

Tulle, silk, viscose, silk organza, georgette, voile

Design notes

Use a 1.5-cm (⅝-in.) seam allowance throughout, unless otherwise stated.

CUTTING GUIDE

1   Front skirt – cut 1 on the fold
2   Back skirt – cut 1 on the fold
3   Waist casing – cut 1 on the fold
4   Front frill – cut 1 on the fold
5   Back frill – cut 1 on the fold
6   Elastic template – do not cut

Finished garment measurements	8	10	12	14	16	18	20	22
Waist (cm)	57.5	62.5	67.5	72.5	77.5	82.5	87.5	92.5
Waist (in.)	22½	24½	26½	28½	30½	32½	34½	36½
Hip (cm)	132	137	142	147	152	157	162	167
Hip (in.)	52	54	56	58	60	62	64	66
Front length (cm)	77.5	77.5	77.5	77.5	77.5	77.5	77.5	77.5
Front length (in.)	30½	30½	30½	30½	30½	30½	30½	30½
Back length (cm)	80	80	80	80	80	80	80	80
Back length (in.)	31½	31½	31½	31½	31½	31½	31½	31½

THE SEWING STARTS HERE

Prepare the pieces

1 Lay out the pattern pieces as shown in the cutting guide. Cut out and transfer any markings to the fabric (see page 37).

Sew the skirt

2 Finish the raw side edges of the front and back skirt pieces. With right sides together, matching the notches, pin and sew the skirt front and back together at the side seams. Press the seams open.

3 Using the elastic template that comes with the pattern, cut the right length of elastic for your size.

4 Attach the waist casing and insert the elastic (see page 197). Slipstitch or machine stitch the gap in the casing closed.

Sew the frill

5 Pin the front and back frills right sides together and sew the short edges together. Press the seams open.

6 Pin hem (see page 42) the bottom edge of the frill.

7 Work two lines of gathering stitches (see page 39) along the top edge of the frill. Gently pull the top threads to gather the frill and distribute the gathers evenly. With right sides together, matching the notches, pin and sew the gathered edge of the frill to the bottom of the skirt. Finish the seam allowances together and press them down towards the hem.

Ra-ra Skirt

Although the design of this skirt harks back to the 1980s, the modern striped fabric brings it right up to date. There are two tiers of ruffles: if you're using a striped fabric like the one shown here, cut them out carefully so that you end up with complete bands of colour when the ruffles are sewn on.

Materials

- 1.6 m (1¾ yd) fabric, 150 cm (60 in.) wide
- 20 cm (8 in.) interfacing
- 23-cm (9-in.) invisible zip
- Basic sewing kit (see page 32)

Difficulty level

Intermediate

Fabric suggestions

Crepe de chine, viscose, silk

Design notes

Use a 1.5-cm (⅝-in.) seam allowance throughout, unless otherwise stated.

Finished garment measurements	8	10	12	14	16	18	20	22
Waist (cm)	70.5	75.5	80.5	85.5	90.5	95.5	100.5	105.5
Waist (in.)	27¾	29¾	31¾	33¾	35¾	37½	39½	41½
Hip (cm)	97.5	102.5	107.5	112.5	117.5	122.5	127.5	132.5
Hip (in.)	38½	40½	42½	44¼	46¼	48¼	50¼	52¼
Front length (cm)	41	41	41	41	41	41	41	41
Front length (in.)	16	16	16	16	16	16	16	16
Back length (cm)	43.5	43.5	43.5	43.5	43.5	43.5	43.5	43.5
Back length (in.)	17	17	17	17	17	17	17	17

CUTTING GUIDE

1 Front waist facing – cut 1 on the fold in fabric
   and 1 on the fold in interfacing

2 Front skirt – cut 1 pair

3 Front frill 1 – cut 1 on the fold

4 Front frill 2 – cut 1 on the fold

5 Back waist facing – cut 1 pair in fabric
   and 1 pair in interfacing

6 Back skirt – cut 1 pair

7 Back frill 1 – cut 1 pair

8 Back frill 2 – cut 1 on the fold

150 cm (60 in.) wide fabric

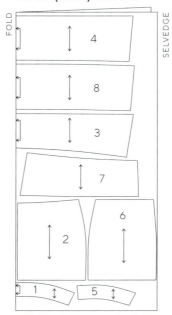

Interfacing

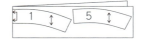

THE SEWING STARTS HERE

Prepare the pieces

1 Lay out the pattern pieces as shown in the cutting guide. Cut out and transfer any markings to the fabric (see page 37).

2 Following the manufacturer's instructions, apply interfacing to the wrong side of the front and back waist facings (see page 35).

Assemble the skirt

3 Pin and stitch the waist darts on the front and back skirts (see page 42). Press the front darts towards the side seams and the back darts towards the centre back.

4 With right sides together and notches matching, pin and sew the centre front seam of the front skirt. Finish the seam allowances and press the seam open.

5 With right sides together, pin and sew the back skirts to the front skirt at the side seams. Finish the seam allowances and press the seams open.

6 Finish the raw edges of the centre back pieces.

7 Insert the invisible zip in the centre back (see page 155).

8 Starting from the hem, pin and sew the centre back seam, stopping at the last zip stitch.

Finish the waistline

9 Attach the waist facing (see page 145). To keep it in place, stitch from the top to the bottom of the facing at the side seams, stitching 'in the ditch' (see page 40).

Hem the skirt

10 Finish the raw bottom edge of the skirt. Fold 1.5 cm (⅝ in.) to the wrong side and press. Stitch in place.

11 With right sides together, pin one back frill 1 piece to each end of front frill 1. Sew together, finish the seam allowances and press the seams open. Finish the top, bottom and centre back edges of the frill with narrow rolled hems (see page 42).

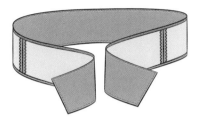

12 Sew two lines of gathering stitches (see page 39) along the top edge of the frill, then gently pull the top threads to gather the fabric. Starting and ending 1 cm (⅜ in.) from the centre back edges and referring to the pattern for the position, pin the gathered edge around the skirt. The ruffles will form a slight dip at the centre front, which you can exaggerate if you wish). Adjust the gathers to ensure they're even, then stitch the frill onto the skirt.

13 With right sides together, pin and sew front frill 2 to back frill 2 at the short edges. Press the seams open. Finish the top and bottom edges of the frill with narrow rolled hems (see page 42). Gather and attach the frill to the skirt, as in step 12.

14 Carefully unpick the gathering stitches from the frills and give the skirt a final press.

Pleats
and Darts

Pleats add volume and wearing ease in a garment; they allow freedom of movement, as they are sewn only across the top to hold them in place. There are various styles of pleat, two of which (box and knife pleats) are shown in this section. We've also included a 'faux' pleat design that does away with the need for fiddly folding. Darts serve the opposite function: they bring the garment in at points such as the bust and waist to provide shaping and a more tailored fit. To explain the principle, this section features the very simplest form of dart for beginners to practise – a waist dart on an A-line skirt – although darts are also used in many other garments in this book.

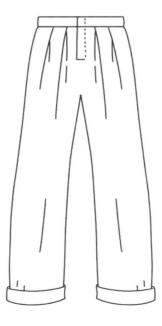

Oxford Bags

Knife pleats at the waist of these trousers provide a sculpted, tailored look over the tummy but add volume over the hips – a flattering style for wider hips.

Materials

- 3 m (3⅜ yd) main fabric, 150 cm (60 in.) wide
- 70 cm (28 in.) interfacing
- 23-cm (9-in.) closed metal zip
- Hook and bar fastening
- Basic sewing kit (see page 32)
- Flat hook and bar or trouser hook and bar

Difficulty level

Intermediate

Fabric suggestions

Cotton sateen, linen blends, viscose twill, lightweight garbadine

Design notes

Use a 1.5-cm (⅝-in.) seam allowance throughout, unless otherwise stated.

Finished garment measurements	8	10	12	14	16	18	20	22
Waist (cm)	80	85	90	95	100	105	110	115
Waist (in.)	31½	33½	35½	37½	39½	41½	43¼	45¼
Hip (cm)	107	112	117	122	127	132	137	142
Hip (in.)	42	44	46	48	50	52	54	56
Inside leg (cm)	78	78	78	78	78	78	78	78
Inside leg (in.)	30¾	30¾	30¾	30¾	30¾	30¾	30¾	30¾

CUTTING GUIDE

150 cm (60 in.) wide fabric

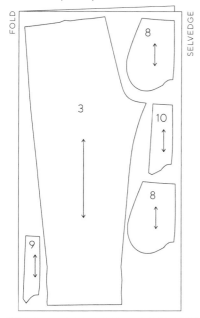

Interfacing

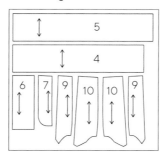

Single layer

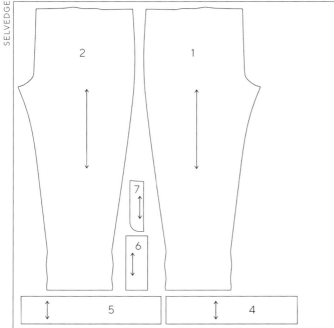

1   Right front trouser – cut 1

2   Left front trouser – cut 1

3   Back trouser – cut 1 pair

4   Left waistband – cut 1
    in fabric and 1 in interfacing

5   Right waistband – cut 1
    in fabric and 1 in interfacing

6   Fly guard – cut 1 in fabric
    and 1 in interfacing

7   Fly facing – cut 1 in fabric
    and 1 in interfacing

8   Pocket bag – cut 2 pairs

9   Front pocket bag facing – cut 1 pair
    in fabric and 1 pair in interfacing

10   Back pocket bag facing – cut 1 pair
     in fabric and 1 pair in interfacing

THE SEWING STARTS HERE

Prepare the pieces

1 Lay out the pattern pieces as shown in the cutting guide. Cut out and transfer any markings to the fabric (see page 37).

2 Following the manufacturer's instructions, apply interfacing to the wrong side of the waistbands, the fly guard and fly facing, and the pocket bag facings (see page 35). Finish the raw edges of the front and back trouser pieces all around.

Insert the fly zip

3 Pin the front trouser pieces right sides together along the crotch seam. Stitch from the bottom of the crotch to the notch for the fly opening.

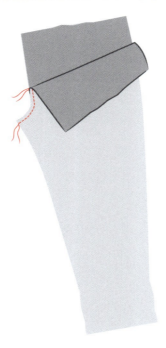

4 Insert the fly zip (see Special Technique: Fly Zip, page 130).

Assemble the trousers

5 Pin and sew the waist darts in the back trouser pieces (see page 42). Press the darts towards the centre back.

6 Place the back pieces right sides together along the centre back seam. Pin, stitch, then press the seam allowances open.

7 From the right side, fold the pleats towards the fly front, then press and tack (baste) in place, tacking within the seam allowance.

SPECIAL TECHNIQUE: FLY ZIP

A fly zip is similar in construction to a lapped zip (see page 117) – it just has an additional shield stitched on the inside. In women's trousers (shown here), the fly fastens right over left; in men's trousers, it's left over right.

The key components of a fly zip are:

Fly facing

The facing covers the zip from view. In some patterns it is cut as a separate piece, as shown here; in others, the facing is an extension of the centre front and is simply folded back.

Fly guard

This double layer of fabric sits between you and the zip and is sewn into the left-hand side of the fly, extending underneath the opening. It stops the zip teeth from catching on your skin when you pull the zip up and down.

1   Overlock (serge) the curved edge of the fly facing only; try not to take any fabric off with your overlocker. Pin the fly facing on the left-hand side of the trouser front (as you look at it), right sides together. Pin and sew from the waist to the zip notch.

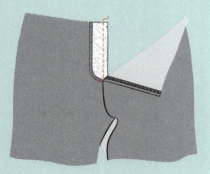

2   Press the facing away from the left trouser leg, then trim the seam allowances and press it away from the trouser leg as well. Place the zip face down on the facing, aligning the bottom of the zip with the zip notch. Align the side of the zip with the seam that joins the facing to the trousers. Sew the right side of the zip to the facing, then fold the facing towards the inside of the trousers and press lightly.

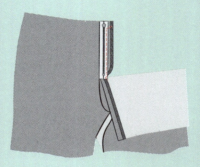

3   Fold the fly guard in half, right sides together. Sew the short curved edge, trim and clip the seam allowances, then turn right side out. Overlock the longest straight edge.

4 Open the zip. Places the trousers right side up, then press 6 mm (¼ in.) to the wrong side on the right-hand side trouser front (as you look at it). Tack (baste) the zip in place behind the fold; you should only see the zip teeth. Position the fly guard behind the trousers, aligning the overlocked edge with the edge of the zip tape and stitch close to the trouser front fold through all three layers (trousers, zip and fly guard).

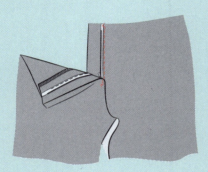

5 Turn the trousers over so that you can see the inside. Pin the fly guard out of the way to prepare for topstitching. Close the zip and turn the trousers right side up again.

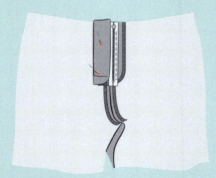

6 Draw a topstitching curve that matches the shape of the fly facing underneath and sew through the trousers and facing.

7 Unpin the fly guard so that it sits over the zip. Pin the fly guard in position where it wants to sit. From the front of the trousers, bar tack at the very bottom of the topstitched line and also at the start of the curve. These stitches will go through all layers: trousers, zip, facing and fly guard.

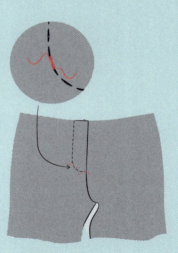

TOP TIP

A bar tack is simply a series of zigzag stitches placed very close together. Set a standard zigzag stitch 2–3mm (¹⁄₁₆–⅛ in.) wide and stitch a short row 1–2 cm (⅜–¾ in.) long. Backstitch once or twice over the entire row to secure.

Attach the side-seam pockets

8 Finish the raw edges around the curved parts of the pocket bags. Place one pocket bag facing on each pocket bag (both right side up), pin together, then zigzag down the long straight edge of the facing. Repeat with the remaining pocket bags and facings, then put them together in pairs – one narrow and one wide facing in each pair.

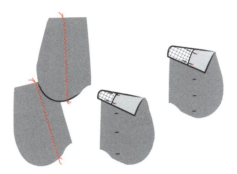

9 Take the two pocket bags with the wider facings. With right sides together, pin one to each side of the back trouser pieces. Taking an 8-mm (5⁄16-in.) seam allowance, stitch from the waistline to 1 cm (3⁄8 in.) from the bottom of the pocket bag.

10 Attach the pocket bags with the narrower facings to the front trouser pieces in the same way.

11 Press both sets of pocket bags away from the leg pieces. Then pin and stitch the front and back pocket bags right sides together around the curved edge.

12 With right sides together, pin the side seams above and below the pocket opening. Stitch from the waistline to the top pocket notch and backstitch to secure. Then stitch from the second pocket notch down to the hem edge.

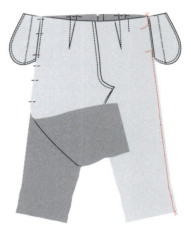

13 Press the side seams open. Press the pocket bags towards the front leg pieces. Tack the pocket bags in place along the waist at the front.

Sew the inside leg seams

14 With right sides together, matching the crotch seams and notches, pin and sew the inside leg seams. Press the seam allowances open.

Sew the turn-ups

15 Sew the turn-ups at the bottom of the trouser legs (see Special Technique: Sewing Turn-ups, page 65).

Attach the waistband

16 Pin the front and back waistbands right sides together at the centre back seam. Stitch together, then press the seam open.

17 Fold the long, un-notched edge of the waistband to the wrong side by 1 cm (⅜ in.) and press. With right sides together, matching the notches to the centre back seam and side seams, pin the waistband to the top of the trousers; at the centre front, both ends of the waistband will extend by 1 cm (⅜ in.).

18 Stitch the waistband in place. Press the seam up.

19 Fold the waistband in half widthways, right sides together. Taking a 1-cm (⅜-in.) seam allowance, stitch across each short end of the waistband, catching in the pressed-up section at the bottom.

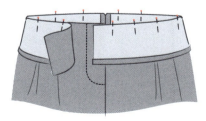

20 Clip the corners of the seam you have just stitched, then turn the waistband right side out. Pin in place from the right side; the folded unstitched edge of the waistband should sit just below the waist seam. Stitch 'in the ditch' (see page 40) around the waist, making sure you catch the folded edge of the waistband in the stitching.

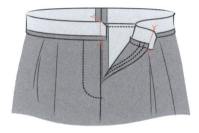

21 Attach the hook part of the fastening to the right waistband and the bar to the left waistband.

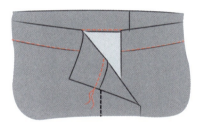

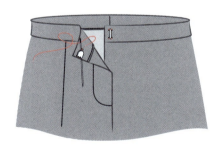

VERSION 2

Pleated Dress

Box pleats at the waistline allow the skirt to gently flare out, creating a soft silhouette that's extremely flattering. Here, the skirt is paired with a fitted, princess-seamed bodice, but it would work equally well on its own.

Materials

- Sizes 8–14: 2.7 m (3 yd) fabric, 150 cm (60 in.) wide
  Sizes 16-22: 3 m (3⅜ yd) fabric, 150 cm (60 in.) wide
- 50 cm (20 in.) interfacing
- 56-cm (22-in.) invisible zip
- 60 cm (24 in.) elastic, 1.2 cm (½ in.) wide,
- Basic sewing kit (see page 32)
- Invisible zip foot

Difficulty level

Intermediate

Fabric suggestions

Viscose twill, cotton or viscose sateen, chambray, crepe-backed satin

Design notes

Use a 1.5-cm (⅝-in.) seam allowance throughout, unless otherwise stated.

Finished garment measurements	8	10	12	14	16	18	20	22
Bust (cm)	89	94	99	104	109	114	119	124
Bust (in.)	35	37	39	41	43	45	47	49
Waist (cm)	73	78	83	88	93	98	103	108
Waist (in.)	28¾	30¾	32¾	34¾	36½	38½	40½	42½
Sleeve length (cm)	39	39.5	40	40.5	41	41.5	42	42.5
Sleeve length (in.)	15¼	15½	15¾	16	16¼	16½	16½	16¾
Front length (cm)	112.5	113	113.5	114	115	115.5	116	116.5
Front length (in.)	44¼	44½	44¾	45	45¼	45½	45¾	46
Back length (cm)	110.5	111	111.5	112	113	113.5	114	114.5
Back length (in.)	43½	43¾	44	44	44½	44¾	45	45

CUTTING GUIDE

Sizes 8-14: 150 cm (60 in.) wide fabric

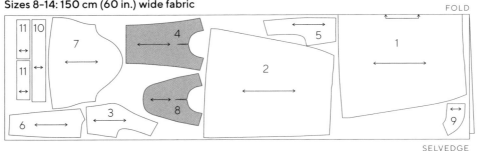

Interfacing

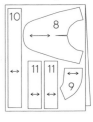

Sizes 16-22: 150 cm (60 in.) wide fabric

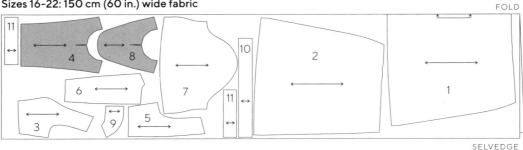

1 Skirt front – cut 1 on the fold

2 Skirt back – cut 1 pair

3 Front bodice side panel – cut 1 pair

4 Front bodice centre panel – cut 1

5 Back bodice side panel – cut 1 pair

6 Back bodice centre panel – cut 1 pair

7 Sleeve – cut 1 pair

8 Front neck facing – cut 1 in fabric and 1 in interfacing

9 Back neck facing – cut 1 pair in fabric and 1 pair in interfacing

10 Front waistband – cut 1 pair in fabric and 1 pair in interfacing

11 Back waistband – cut 2 pairs in fabric and 2 pairs in interfacing

THE SEWING STARTS HERE

Prepare the pieces

1 Lay out the pattern pieces as shown in the cutting guide. Cut out and transfer any markings to the fabric (see page 37).

2 Following the manufacturer's instructions, apply interfacing to the wrong side of the facings and waistbands (see page 35).

3 Stay stitch (see page 40) the front and back necklines. Finish (see page 38) the raw side edges of all the bodice pieces.

Assemble the front and back bodices

4 With right sides together, matching the notches, pin one front bodice side panel to each side of the centre panel. Stitch together, snip into the seam allowances at the curves (see page 39) and press the seams open.

5 Repeat step 4 with the back side and centre bodice pieces.

6 With right sides together, matching the princess seams, pin the front and back bodices together at the shoulders. Stitch together, finish the seam allowances and press the seams open. Finish the side edges. With right sides together and notches matching, pin and stitch the front and back bodices together at the side edges. Press the seams open.

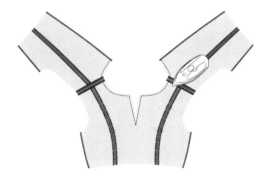

Insert the sleeves

7 Finish the raw edges around the sleeves and bodice armholes. Sew a line of gathering stitches (see page 39) between the notches on the sleeve caps. Carefully pull the top threads to create gathers.

8 Fold the sleeves in half, right sides together, and pin and stitch the underarm seams. Press the seams open. Turn the sleeves right side out.

9 With right sides together, matching the notches, slot the sleeves into the armholes, making sure the underarm and bodice side seams match. Pin in place. Distribute the gathers evenly between the notches, then sew the sleeves in place. Press the seams towards the sleeves.

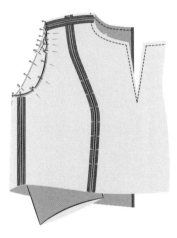

10 At the end of the sleeves, fold 6 mm (¼ in.) followed by a further 2 cm (¾ in.) to the wrong side and press. Edge stitch close to the fold, leaving a 5-cm (2-in.) gap, to form a casing for the elastic.

11 Wrap elastic around your elbow and measure a length that feels comfortable. Add 2 cm (¾ in.), then cut two pieces of elastic to that length. Attach a safety pin to one end of the elastic, then feed it through the channel. Overlap the ends of the elastic by 1 cm (⅜ in.) and zigzag stitch across the elastic to create a loop. Tuck the elastic inside the casing. Stitch the gap in the casing closed.

Sew the waistbands

12 With right sides together, pin one set of back waistband pieces to a front waistband at the side seams. Stitch, then press the seams open. Finish the raw centre back edges. Repeat with the remaining waistband pieces.

13 Fold under and press 1.2 cm (½ in.) to the wrong side at the bottom edge of one of the waistbands; this will be the inner waistband.

14 With right sides together, matching the seams and notches, pin the outer waistband around the bottom edge of the bodice. Then pin the right side of the inner waistband to the wrong side of the bodice, so that the bodice is sandwiched in between the two waistbands. Stitch, grade the seam allowances (see page 39), then press the waistbands down, away from the bodice..

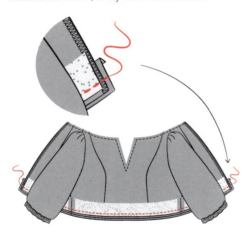

Sew the skirt

15 Finish the raw side edges of the skirt pieces and the centre back edges of the back skirt. Pin the front and back skirt pieces right sides together at the side seams. Sew together, then press the seams open.

16 Locate the notches for the pleats at the top edge of the skirt and fold them in place. Press and pin the pleats in place (see Special Technique: Pleats, see page 140); the pleats in this dress are box pleats. Tack (baste) the pleats in place by hand or machine, stitching within the seam allowance.

Join the skirt and bodice

17 With right sides together, pin the top edge of the skirt to the bottom edge of the outer waistband and stitch in place. Do not attach the inner waistband – hold or pin it out of the way while you stitch. Grade the seam allowances, then press the seam up.

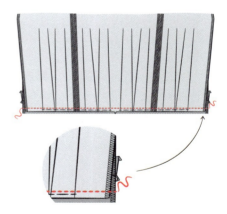

18 Bring the inner waistband down to cover the seam allowances and pin it in place from the right side of the dress. Stitch 'in the ditch' (see page 40) around the bodice and waistband.

Insert the zip

19 Insert the invisible zip in the centre back (see page 155). Sew the rest of the centre back seam from the zip notch down to the hem.

Finish the neckline

20 Join the front and back neck facings at the shoulder, then attach the facing to the bodice (see page 44). Carefully grade and clip into the curved seam allowance. Understitch (see page 40) the seam allowances to the facing. Finish the curved edges of the facing pieces.

(see page 155)

TOP TIP

Mark the seam allowances on the centre front of the neckline as a stitching guide; this will help you get a really neat finish when you turn the facing to the inside of the garment.

21 Change to a zip foot. Line up the short centre back edges of the facing pieces with the back bodice seam allowances and pin in place over the zip. Sew in place, stitching close to the zip teeth. Snip the corners of the seam allowances and turn the facing to the wrong side to expose the zip coil. Press the back bodice, avoiding the zip coil.

22 Turn the facing to the wrong side of the garment and press carefully.

23 Around the hem of the skirt, fold and press 6 mm (¼ in.) followed by a further 2.5 cm (1 in.) to the wrong side and press. Pin in place, then stitch as close as possible to the folded edge.

SPECIAL TECHNIQUE: PLEATS

Pleats are a way of adding and controlling volume in a garment. You will often find them around the waist on blouses, dresses, skirts and trousers (pants). The method used determines how much volume you can add.

Knife pleats

Knife pleats are equal folds on the inside and the outside, all facing in the same direction.

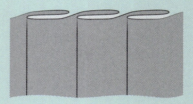

Box pleats

Box pleats consist of two knife pleats that face away from each other. The volume sits on the outside of this pleat.

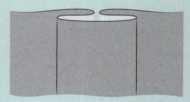

Inverted box pleats

These are the same as box pleats, but in reverse: the two knife pleats face towards each other. The volume sits on the inside of this pleat.

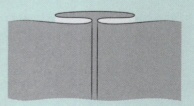

TOP TIP

To ensure that multiple pleats are even, use a pleat template, which is easy to make from a strip of card. Having determined the width of the fabric to be taken in the pleat, cut a card strip to this width. On one long edge, mark 'Placement Line'; on the other long edge, mark 'Fold Line'. Place the card on the right side of the fabric to be pleated and mark the two lines, using a different colour for each.

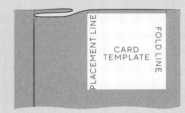

Constructing pleats

1 Pleat lines on your pattern are indicated by two lines and an arrow for the direction in which to fold the pleat. The line that the arrow is pointing to is called the Placement Line; the other line is the Fold Line. Fold the fabric at the Fold Line mark and bring it to the Placement Line mark, keeping the raw edges of the fabric even. The pleat formed will be half the width of the marked fabric.

PATTERN MARKINGS FOR A KNIFE PLEAT

2 For pleats that are functional rather than decorative (like a waist pleat), the pleats are only pinned and pressed right at the edge, so they can be sewn into the seam. We recommend machine tacking (basting) them down within the seam allowance. The rest of the pleat creates volume in the garment. Some garments have pleats along the entire length of the garment for decoration and volume (like a pleated skirt), in which case you press the entire pleat to make it lie flat.

PATTERN MARKINGS FOR A BOX PLEAT

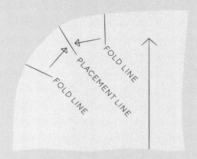

3 Machine tack (baste) across the top of the pleats to hold them in place, tacking within the seam allowance. You can also stitch down the 2–3 cm (1 in. or so) of the pleat to create a flatter shape; to do this, stitch very close to the folded edge of the pleat.

4 To keep pleats folded in place, working from the wrong side, machine stitch close to the inner fold, particularly in the hem area.

5 Press your pleats very carefully if you are pressing them in! Place a pressing cloth in between the iron and the garment to prevent the pleat indentations showing on the garment.

Wool Mini Skirt

If you're new to sewing and looking for a garment that is simple to sew but perfectly fitted, then the waist darts in this mini skirt make it the perfect beginner's project. Made from wool fabric, which is both easy to sew and not prone to fraying or stretching, it has deep patch pockets trimmed with piping that's similar in colour to the skirt but adds a subtle contrast in texture. The waist facing gives a neat and tidy finish but is simple to apply.

Materials

- 80 cm (32 in.) fabric, 150 cm (60 in.) wide
- 30 cm (12 in.) interfacing
- 3 m (3⅜ yd) 5-mm (³⁄₁₆-in.) corded piping
- 22.5-cm (9-in.) closed-end zip
- Basic sewing kit (see page 32)

Difficulty level

Intermediate

Fabric suggestions

Washed wool, cashmere crepe, jacquard, corduroy

Design notes

Use a 1.5-cm (⅝-in.) seam allowance throughout, unless otherwise stated.

The pockets can be in a contrast fabric. For the piping on the pockets, you can either make your own or buy flanged piping, which already has the fabric attached.

The seam edges of the skirt do not need to be finished; they can be left raw if your fabric does not fray.

Finished garment measurements	8	10	12	14	16	18	20	22
Waist (cm)	66.5	71.5	76.5	81.5	86.5	91.5	96.5	101.5
Waist (in.)	26	28	30	32	34	36	38	40
Hip (cm)	96	101	106	111	116	121	126	131
Hip (in.)	37¾	39¾	41¾	43¾	45¾	47¾	49¾	51¾
Finished length (cm)	45	45	45	45	45	45	45	45
Finished length (in.)	17¾	17¾	17¾	17¾	17¾	17¾	17¾	17¾

CUTTING GUIDE

150 cm (60 in.) wide fabric

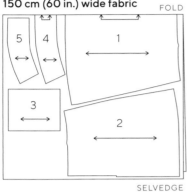

Interfacing

1   Front skirt – cut 1 on fold

2   Back skirt – cut 1 pair

3   Pocket – cut 1 pair

4   Front waist facing – cut 1 on fold in fabric and 1 on fold in interfacing

5   Back waist facing – cut 1 pair in fabric and 1 pair in interfacing

THE SEWING STARTS HERE

Prepare the pieces

1   Lay out the pattern pieces as shown in the cutting guide. Cut out and transfer any markings to the fabric (see page 37). Also cut a rectangle for the pocket measuring 23 x 19 cm (9 x 7½ in.).

2   Following the manufacturer's instructions, apply interfacing to the wrong side of the front and back waist facings (see page 35).

Sew the darts

3   Pin and sew the darts on the front skirt (see page 42). Press the darts towards the side seams.

Sew the pockets

4   Along the top edge of each pocket, press 3 cm (1¼ in.) to the wrong side. Topstitch 2 cm (¾ in.) from the fold to hold the pocket edge in place.

5   Around the side and bottom edges, press 1 cm (⅜ in.) to the wrong side.

6   Open up the pressed seam allowances and pin the corded piping to the right side of the pockets, aligning the edge of the piping with the crease lines. Stitch in place, using a zip foot to stitch as close to the piping as possible.

SPECIAL TECHNIQUE: WAIST FACING

Facings are shaped sections of fabrics that finish off the raw edges of clothes at the neckline, waist, armholes and even hems. Once attached, a facing is turned to the inside of a garment, so is invisible from the outside. Waist facings add stability around the waistline and stop them from stretching over time.

1 Open up the zip on the garment. With right sides together, pin the facing to the garment around the waistline, matching up the side seams and matching the darts with the corresponding notches on the facing. Stitch in place. Clip into the seam allowance around the waist. Press the facing and seam allowances away from the waistline.

2 Understitch all around the facing, just above the seam line at the waist (see page 40); you're stitching the seam allowance to the facing only. This will stop the facing from rolling out from the inside. Start and end this stitching 2.5 cm (1 in.) away from the zip.

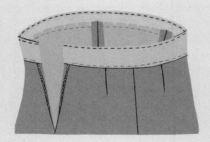

3 Change the regular sewing foot to a zip foot. Fold down and line up the short edges of the facing pieces with the seam allowance and pin in place over the zip. Sew in place by stitching close to the zip teeth.

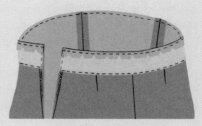

4 Tuck your thumb into the corner at the top of the zip and, folding the layers around your thumb, turn the facing through to the right side, wrapping it over to the wrong side of the garment. Once it's turned through, press to create a really sharp corner and press around the waistline to create a neat top edge.

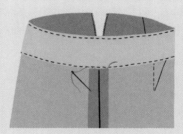

5 Hand stitch the facing to the side seams, centre front and centre back of the garment. This will keep the facing on the inside of the garment when worn.

TOP TIPS

- Remember to leave extra piping cord at the start and end.
- You may need to snip into the piping fabric at the pocket corners to enable it to lie flat.

....

7 Fold the seam allowance to the wrong side of the pocket, tucking the excess piping over the top edge.

8 Place the pockets on the right side of the skirt front in the positions marked on the pattern. Stitch in place. Press the pockets.

Sew the back skirt pieces

9 Pin and sew the darts on the back skirt pieces. Press the darts towards the centre back.

10 Place the back pieces right sides together and pin together along the centre back from the hem up to the zip notch. Stitch up to the zip notch.

11 Snip into the seam allowances at the zip notch on a diagonal, then press the seam allowances open.

12 With both skirt and zip right side up, tuck the snipped triangle of fabric inwards, then place the zip underneath the centre back opening and pin it in place so that it sits flat and the teeth are exposed. The zip teeth should sit 1.5 cm (⅝ in.) below the top edge to allow for the waistband facing seam allowance. Topstitch the zip in place.

13 Place the front and back skirt pieces right sides together, then pin and stitch the side seams. Press the seams open.

Sew and attach the waist facing

14 Place the front and back waist facings right sides together, matching the raw short edges. Pin and stitch together at the side seams. Press the seams open.

15 Attach the facing to the waistline of the skirt (see Special Technique: Waist Facing, page 145).

16 Press the hem of the skirt to the wrong side by 3 cm (1¼ in.). Pin in place, then stitch all the way around, 2 cm (¾ in.) from the fold.

VERSION 4

Faux Pleat Dress

At first glance, this dress looks as if it has a vertical pleat running down the side of the princess seam line, but it's actually a separate panel, interfaced to give it some body. Made in a luxurious jacquard fabric, it's a dramatic design that is guaranteed to turn heads!

Materials

○ Sizes 8–14: 2.6 m (2⅞ yd) fabric, 150 cm (60 in.) wide
   Sizes 16–22: 3.2 m (3½ yd) fabric, 150 cm (60 in.) wide

○ 80 cm (32 in.) lining fabric, 150 cm (60 in.) wide

○ 1.3 m (1½ yd) interfacing

○ 56-cm (22-in.) invisible zip

○ Basic sewing kit (see page 32)

Difficulty level

Intermediate

Fabric suggestions

Jacquard, denim, African wax fabric, linen blends, brocade, dupioni

Design notes

Use a 1.5-cm (⅝-in.) seam allowance throughout, unless otherwise stated.

Finished garment measurements	8	10	12	14	16	18	20	22
Bust (cm)	89	94	99	104	109	114	119	124
Bust (in.)	35	37	39	41	43	45	47	49
Waist (cm)	77	82	87	92	97	102	107	112
Waist (in.)	30¼	32¼	34¼	36¼	38¼	40¼	42¼	44
Hip (cm)	95	100	105	110	115	120	125	130
Hip (in.)	37½	39½	41½	43¼	45¼	47¼	49¼	51¼
Sleeve length (cm)	59	59.5	60	60.5	61	61.5	62	62.5
Sleeve length (in.)	23¼	23½	23¾	23¾	24	24¼	24½	24¾
Front length (cm)	87.5	88	88.5	89	90	90.5	91	91.5
Front length (in.)	34½	34¾	35	35	35½	35¾	36	36
Back length (cm)	84.5	85	85.5	86	87	87.5	88	88.5
Back length (in.)	33¼	33½	33¾	34	34¼	34½	34½	34¾

CUTTING GUIDE

Sizes 8–14: 150 cm (60 in.) wide fabric

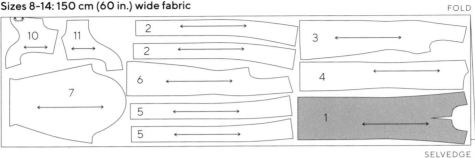

FOLD

SELVEDGE

Sizes 16–22: 150 cm (60 in.) wide fabric

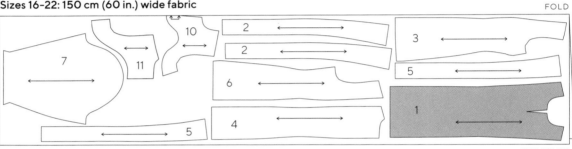

FOLD

SELVEDGE

Sizes 8–14: Lining

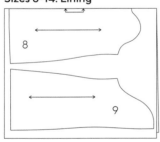

Sizes 16–22: Lining

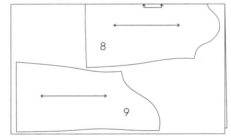

Interfacing

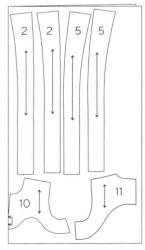

1 Centre front – cut 1

2 Front faux pleat panel – cut 2 pairs in fabric and 2 pairs in interfacing

3 Side front – cut 1 pair

4 Centre back – cut 1 pair

5 Back faux pleat panel – cut 2 pairs in fabric and 2 pairs in interfacing

6 Side back – cut 1 pair

7 Sleeve – cut 1 pair

8 Front lining – cut 1 on the fold

9 Back lining – cut 1 pair

10 Front neck facing – cut 1 on the fold in fabric and 1 on the fold in interfacing

11 Back neck facing – cut 1 pair in fabric and 1 pair in interfacing

THE SEWING STARTS HERE

Prepare the pieces

1 Lay out the pattern pieces as shown in the cutting guide. Cut out and transfer any markings to the fabric (see page 37).

2 Following the manufacturer's instructions, apply interfacing to the wrong side of all the faux pleat panel pieces and the facings (see page 35). Label each piece so that you can differentiate the front pieces from the back.

3 Stay stitch (see page 40) the front and back necklines.

Construct the faux pleat panels

The interfaced faux pleat panels are stitched together before they are attached to the princess seam lines.

4 With right sides together, matching the notches, pin one front faux pleat panel to a back faux pleat panel at the shoulder seams and stitch them together. Press the seam open. Repeat with the remaining faux pleat panel pieces.

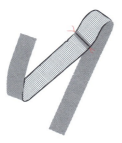

TOP TIP

Since there are so many pieces to work with, it is important to mark your pieces correctly so that you can differentiate between the front and back pieces. One option is to mark them with chalk or an erasable fabric marker; alternatively, use different-coloured stickers or washi tape to tell them apart. Also, make your markings close to the shoulder edges.

5 You now have four very long strips. Place them in pairs, right sides together: one side of each pair will form the outer layer of the faux pleats and one side the inner layer. Matching the notches and shoulder seams, stitch each pair together along the edge with four single notches and along both short ends, leaving the straighter long edge open.

6 Trim the seam allowances, turn the panel right side out along the seam line and press. You now have two very long strips, each consisting of two interfaced layers.

Assemble the side and front/back panels

7 On the side front pieces, mark and sew the bust darts (see page 42). Press the darts down towards the hem.

8 Insert the invisible zip in the centre back (see page 155). Complete the centre back seam by sewing from the last zip stitch down to the hem.

9 With right sides together, pin and sew the side front pieces to the side back pieces at the shoulders. Then sew the centre front piece to the centre back pieces at the shoulders as well. Trim the seam allowances to reduce bulk and press the seams open.

Insert the faux pleats

10 Matching the notches and shoulder seams, place the side and front/back panels right sides together and sandwich the raw edges of the faux pleat panels in between. Pin and sew in place. Press the seams open – there's no need to finish them at this point.

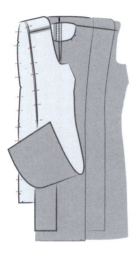

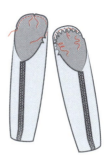

14 Turn the sleeves right side out. With right sides together, matching the double and single notches, insert the sleeves into the armholes. Adjust the gathers to fit if necessary. Pin and sew in place (see page 43).

Insert the lining

15 At the top edge of the front lining, sew 2 rows of gathering stitches. This is to help ease in the top edge of the lining piece to the bottom edge of the front facing. With right sides together, pin the bottom edge of the front neck facing to the top edge of the front lining. The edges of both pieces are very curved, so start pinning from the notches and move on to ease in the rest of the fabric. You can also snip into the curves if the fabric feels difficult to ease in. Sew both pieces together, snip into the curved seam allowance and press the seam open. Repeat with the back lining and facing pieces.

TOP TIP

Note that the bottom edge of the faux pleat panels will end slightly above the hem of the dress.

11 With right sides together, matching the notches, pin and sew the side seams. Press the seams open.

Insert the sleeves

12 With right sides together, matching the notches, fold the sleeves in half and pin and stitch the underarm seams. Finish the raw edges and press the seams open.

13 Around the sleeve head, sew two rows of gathering stitches (see page 39). Carefully pull the top threads to create gathers. The back of the sleeve will be gathered from the middle notch to the double notch by 12 cm (4¾ in.) and the front of the sleeve from the middle notch to the single notch by 7 cm (2¾ in.).

16 With right sides together, pin and sew the front lining piece to the back lining pieces at the shoulders. Press the seams open.

17 With right sides together, pin the facing portion of the lining to the dress around the neckline. Mark the stitching line, then sew around the neckline from one centre back edge to the other, carefully pivoting at the V-point of the neckline. Snip into the seam allowance at the V as close as possible to the stitching, then trim and grade the seam allowances (see page 39), trimming the facing side of the seam the most.

18 Understitch (see page 40) the seam allowance to the lining as far as you can go into the V neckline. Start understitching again into the other side of the V. Fold the lining to the wrong side of the dress and press the neckline.

19 With right sides together, pin the lining to the main fabric at the centre back edges, catching the zip tape. Switch over to your zip foot. Working from the main fabric side and stitching 'in the ditch' (see page 40) over the original zip stitching as close to the zip coil as possible, sew from the neckline to the zip notch. Repeat on the other side of the centre back.

20 There will be an opening at the bottom edge of the lining's centre back, below the zip. Pin both edges right sides together and sew all the way down to the hem. Press the seam open.

21 Fold the dress out of the way. With right sides together, matching the notches, pin and stitch the side seams of the lining from the armhole down to the hem. Press the seams open.

22 With wrong sides together, pin the lining to the armhole seam allowances and stitch all around 1 cm (⅜ in.) from the raw edge. Finish this seam allowance's raw edges.

23 Finish the sleeve hems and fold them over to the wrong side by 1 cm (⅜ in.). Press and sew in place.

24 Finish the bottom edge of the lining fabric. Turn the bottom edge of the lining to the wrong side by 1.5 cm (⅝ in.) and pin and sew in place.

25 Finish the bottom edge of the dress. Turn the bottom edge to the wrong side by 1.5 cm (⅝ in.) and pin and sew in place. Note that you're leaving the bottom edge of the lining loose – do not pin the dress hem over it.

SPECIAL TECHNIQUE: INVISIBLE ZIP

An invisible zip differs from a regular zip, as the teeth are on the underside of the zip tape with just the little zip pull showing on the right side. You will need a special invisible zip foot, which has two angled curves on the underside that hold the zip teeth to one side of the needle, allowing you to stitch close to the zip. Invisible zips are inserted from the top down and are applied to an open seam, on the seam allowances only.

If you have a waist seam in the middle of your zip, start at step 1; if not, start at step 2.

1 Position the zip tape along the centre back of the garment and make a small mark on each side of the zip tape where it matches the waist seam. The top edge of the zip tape should reach the top of your garment.

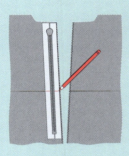

2 Unzip your zip and iron the teeth slightly away from the tape to make it easier to attach. Use a cool setting or the zip will melt.

3 With the garment right side up, lay the right-hand side of the zip tape right side down on the left-hand side of the garment opening. Pin in place, matching the mark you made earlier with the waist seam (if this applies to your garment). If you wish, you can tack (baste) the zip in place.

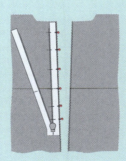

4 Start stitching from the top by slotting the zip teeth into the left groove of the invisible zip foot. Sew as far down as you can; you will have to stop when you reach the zip pull.

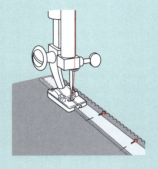

5 Now position and pin the other side of the zip to the remaining side of your garment opening. Be careful not to get the zip twisted.

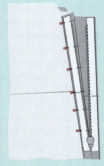

6 Sew from the top down by slotting the zip teeth into the right groove of the invisible zip foot.

7 Test your zip and give your garment a gentle press.

8 Close the zip. Pin the rest of the seam right sides together and stitch with a regular zip foot. You will have to start a little bit above and away from your zip stitch line to avoid the bulk of the zip pull. Also pull out the end of the zip tape so that it's not in the way.

VERSION 5

Faux Pleat Top

This is a shorter version of the dress on page 148, but the softer, patterned broderie anglaise fabric gives it a much less structured and more informal feel.

Difficulty level

Intermediate

Fabric suggestions

Jacquard, denim, African wax fabric, linen blends, brocade, dupioni, cotton poplin, chambray

Design notes

Use a 1.5-cm (⅝-in.) seam allowance throughout, unless otherwise stated.

Materials

- Sizes 8–14: 2 m (2¼ yd) fabric, 150 cm (60 in.) wide
  Sizes 16–22: 2.7 m (3 yd) fabric, 150 cm (60 in.) wide
- 1.3 m (1½ yd) interfacing
- 35-cm (14-in.) invisible zip
- Basic sewing kit (see page 32)
- Invisible zip foot

Finished garment measurements	8	10	12	14	16	18	20	22
Bust (cm)	89	94	99	104	109	114	119	124
Bust (in.)	35	37	39	41	43	45	47	49
Waist (cm)	77	82	87	92	97	102	107	112
Waist (in.)	30¼	32¼	34¼	36¼	38¼	40¼	42¼	44
Hip (cm)	95	100	105	110	115	120	125	130
Hip (in.)	37½	39½	41½	43¼	45¼	47¼	49¼	51¼
Sleeve length (cm)	59	59.5	60	60.5	61	61.5	62	62.5
Sleeve length (in.)	23¼	23½	23¾	23¾	24	24¼	24½	24¾
Front length (cm)	60.5	61	61.5	62	62.5	63.5	64	64.5
Front length (in.)	23¾	24	24¼	24½	24¾	25	25¼	25½
Back length (cm)	56.5	57	57.5	58	59	59.5	60	60.5
Back length (in.)	22¼	22½	22¾	22¾	23¼	23½	23¾	23¾

CUTTING GUIDE

1 Centre front – cut 1

2 Front faux pleat panel – cut 2 pairs in fabric and 2 pairs in interfacing

3 Side front – cut 1 pair

4 Centre back – cut 1 pair

5 Back faux pleat panel – cut 2 pairs in fabric and 2 pairs in interfacing

6 Side back – cut 1 pair

7 Sleeve – cut 1 pair

8 Front neck facing – cut 1 on the fold in fabric and 1 on the fold in interfacing

9 Back neck facing – cut 1 pair in fabric and 1 pair in interfacing

THE SEWING STARTS HERE

Make the top following steps 1–14 of the dress, with the following changes:

- In step 5, do not sew the short edges of the faux pleat panels.

- In step 8, finish the raw centre back edges before inserting the zip.

- In step 10, the mid panels will end level with the hem of the top.

- In step 14, finish the sleeve seam allowances after you've sewn the sleeves in place.

- Omit steps 15–22 (the lining); instead, sew and attach a neck facing (see page 44).

- In step 23, fold the sleeve hems over to the wrong side by 1 cm (⅜ in.).

- In step 25, turn the bottom edge to the wrong side by 2.5 cm (1 in.).

Sizes 8–14: 150 cm (60 in.) wide fabric

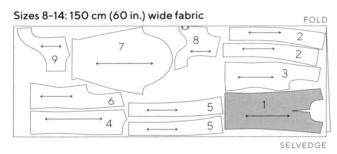

Sizes 16–22: 150 cm (60 in.) wide fabric

Interfacing

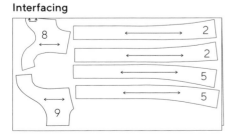

Boat Necklines

A boat neck is a wide neckline that runs across the collarbone, almost to the shoulder points. It is traditionally used in nautically inspired sweaters, but also features in more elegant dresses and evening wear. It's very simple to make slight adjustments to the shape of the neckline – just ensure that any alterations you make are perfectly symmetrical.

Classic Breton Top

This is a classic design – a Breton top in striped jersey fabric with shoulder plackets that provide an attractive decorative details, as well as a means of fastening the top. If you make it in a horizontal stripe, as here, do take the time to ensure that the stripes align on the front and back.

Materials

- 1.2 m (1⅜ yd) fabric, 150 cm (60 in.) wide
- 20 cm (8 in.) interfacing
- 1 m (1 yd) cotton tape
- 3 buttons, 1 cm (⅜ in.) in diameter
- Basic sewing kit (see page 32)

Difficulty level

Confident sewer

Fabric suggestions

Ponte roma, jersey, double knit

Design notes

Use a 1.5-cm (⅝-in.) seam allowance throughout, unless otherwise stated.

Finished garment measurements	8	10	12	14	16	18	20	22
Bust (cm)	76.5	81.5	86.5	91.5	96.5	101.5	106.5	111.5
Bust (in.)	30	32	34	36	38	40	42	44
Sleeve length (cm)	41.5	42	42.5	43	43.5	44	44.5	45
Sleeve length (in.)	16¼	16½	16¾	17	17¼	17¼	17½	17¾
Finished length (cm)	52	52.5	53	53.5	54	55	55.5	56
Finished length (in.)	20½	20¾	21	21	21¼	21¾	22	22

CUTTING GUIDE

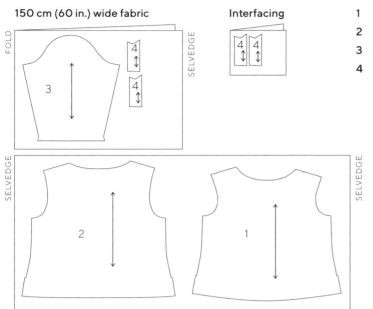

150 cm (60 in.) wide fabric

Interfacing

1 Front – cut 1

2 Back – cut 1

3 Sleeve – cut 1 pair

4 Shoulder placket – cut 2 pairs in fabric and 2 pairs in interfacing

THE SEWING STARTS HERE

Prepare the pieces

1 Lay out the pattern pieces as shown in the cutting guide. Cut out and transfer any markings to the fabric (see page 37).

2 Following the manufacturer's instructions, apply interfacing to the wrong side of the shoulder placket pieces (see page 35).

....

TOP TIP

Remember to match the stripes on the front and back pieces when cutting out, and to make sure that the stripes on the shoulder plackets run horizontally.

....

Sew the right shoulder seam

3 With right sides together, pin the front and back pieces together along the right shoulder seam. Stitch, then finish the seam allowances together and press the seam towards the back.

Construct and attach the shoulder plackets

4 Take each pair of shoulder plackets and pin them right sides together. On the front placket, match the double notches, then pin and stitch along that edge; on the back placket, match the single notches, then pin and stitch along that edge. Taking a 1.5-cm (⅝-in.) seam allowance, stitch along the neck edge of both plackets.

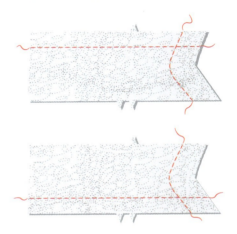

5 Trim the seam allowances, clip the corners, turn the plackets right side out and press flat.

6 With right sides together, matching the notches (see Top Tip on page 166), pin the raw long edges of the plackets to the left shoulder of the front and back pieces at the positions marked on the pattern, leaving a 1.5-cm (⅝-in.) gap at the neck edge. Stitch in place. Press the seam allowances and plackets away from the shoulder.

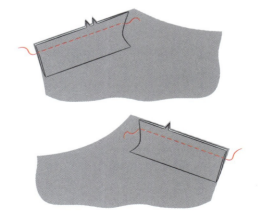

TOP TIP

On the front, match the single notch of the placket with the single notch on the left shoulder; on the back, match the double notches of the placket with the double notches on the left shoulder.

7 The front placket will overlap the back, so mark and stitch the buttonholes on the front placket (see page 48). Do not attach the buttons yet.

Finish the neck edge

8 On the right side of the top, pin cotton tape around the neck edge, aligning the top edge of the tape with the raw edge of the neck. The tape should extend 1 cm (⅜ in.) beyond the start of each shoulder placket. Stitch along the bottom edge of the tape to secure it in place.

9 Turn the neck edge of the top to the wrong side by 1.5 cm (⅝ in.), so that 6 mm (¼ in.) of the top shows above the tape on the inside of the garment. Tuck in the 1-cm (⅜-in.) tape overlaps. Pin in place.

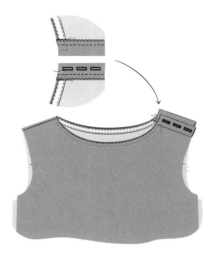

10 Topstitch around the neck 1.2 cm (½ in.) from the neck edge; this will catch the cotton tape at the bottom edge. Press the neck.

11 On the left shoulder, overlap the placket pieces front over back and tack (baste) together at the armhole.

Attach the sleeves

12 With right sides together, matching the notches, pin the sleeves into the armholes. Stitch, then finish the seam allowances together. (Note that you will catch the placket pieces in the stitching at the left shoulder.) Press the seams towards the sleeves.

Sew the underarm and side seams

13 With right sides together, pin the front and back together along the underarm and side seams until you get to the vent point. Stitch from the sleeve hem to the vent point. At the vent point, make a 1.5-cm (⅝-in.) snip into the seam allowance below the last stitch you sewed. Finish the seam allowances together, then press the seams towards the back of the top.

Sew the sleeve hem

14 Press the sleeve hems to the wrong side by 1.5 cm (⅝ in.), then stitch the hems in place.

Sew the side vents

15 Finish each side of the vent, then press to the wrong side by 1.5 cm (⅝ in.). Pin in place.

16 From the right side, stitching 1 cm (⅜ in.) away from the slit, stitch from the hem up to the top of the vent, 6 mm (¼ in.) across the top, and down the other side.

Finishing touches

17 Around the bottom edge, turn 1.5 cm (⅝ in.) to the wrong side. Pin, then topstitch the hem in place from the right side.

18 Mark the button positions on the back placket and stitch the buttons in place..

Cropped Top & Trousers

The neckline is a little narrower and slightly less scooped than that of the Classic Breton Top; the overall silhouette, with shorter sleeves and bodice, is more square and 'boxy'. The striped fabric echoes that of the traditional top, but the stripes run vertically, rather than horizontally. The fabric is less clingy, too, creating a crisper outline. Here we've paired the top with easy-to-make trousers, similar in construction to the pyjamas on pages 194 and 205.

Materials

- Sizes 8–14: 3 m (3⅜ yd) fabric, 150 cm (60 in.) wide
  Sizes 16–22: 3.7 m (4 yd) fabric, 150 cm (60 in.) wide

- 50 cm (20 in.) interfacing

- 2 m (2¼ yd) elastic, 2.5 cm (1 in.) wide

- 25-cm (10-in.) invisible zip

- Basic sewing kit (see page 32)

Difficulty level

Confident sewer

Fabric suggestions

Linen or cotton blends, African wax, chambray, denim

Design notes

Use a 1.5-cm (⅝-in.) seam allowance throughout, unless otherwise stated.

CUTTING GUIDE

Top

1 Front bodice
   – cut 1 on the fold

2 Back bodice
   – cut 1 on the fold

3 Front neck facing
   – cut 1 on the fold in fabric and 1 on the fold in interfacing

4 Back neck facing
   – cut 1 in fabric and 1 in interfacing

5 Sleeve – cut 1 pair

6 Sleeve cuff – cut 1 pair

Trousers

7 Front trouser
   – cut 1 pair

8 Back trouser
   – cut 1 pair

9 Front waist facing
   – cut 1 in fabric and 1 in interfacing

Sizes 8–14: 150 cm (60 in.) wide fabric

Sizes 16–22: 150 cm (60 in.) wide fabric

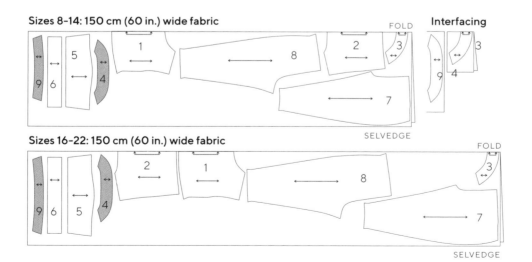

Finished garment measurements

TOP	8	10	12	14	16	18	20	22
Bust (cm)	104	109	114	119	124	129	134	139
Bust (in.)	41	43	45	47	49	51	53	55
Sleeve length (cm)	21	21.5	22	22.5	23	23.5	24	24.5
Sleeve length (in.)	8¼	8½	8¾	9	9	9¼	9½	9¾
Front length (cm)	40.5	41	41.5	42	43	43.5	44	44.5
Front length (in.)	16	16	16¼	16½	17	17¼	17¼	17½
Back length (cm)	35.5	36	36.5	37	38	38.5	39	39.5
Back length (in.)	14	14¼	14½	14½	15	15¼	15	15½

TROUSERS	8	10	12	14	16	18	20	22
Waist (cm)	80	85	90	95	100	105	110	115
Waist (in.)	31½	33½	35½	37½	39½	41½	43¼	45¼
Hip (cm)	99.5	104.5	109.5	114.5	119.5	124.5	129.5	134.5
Hip (in.)	39	41	43	45	47	49	51	53
Inside leg (cm)	69	69	69	69	69	69	69	69
Inside leg (in.)	27	27	27	27	27	27	27	27

TOP

Prepare the pieces

1 Lay out the pattern pieces as shown in the cutting guide. Cut out and transfer any markings to the fabric (see page 37).

2 Following the manufacturer's instructions, apply interfacing to the wrong side of the front and back neck facings (see page 35).

Sew the right shoulder seam

3 With right sides together, pin and sew the front and back pieces together along the shoulder seams. Finish the seam allowances together and press the seams towards the back.

4 Sew the neck facing and attach it to the garment (see page 44).

5 Finish the raw side edges of the front and back bodices. Then finish the two short edges and the top edges of both sleeves.

6 Lay the bodice flat. With right sides together, matching the notches, pin and sew the sleeves to the arm opening. Press the seam open. Repeat with the other sleeve.

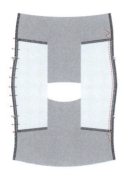

7 Fold the top in half, right sides together. Pin the underarm and side seams, then sew from the sleeve edge to the bodice hem on each side. Press the seams open.

8 With right sides together, and pin and sew the short edges of the cuffs together. Press the seams open, then fold the cuffs in half widthways, wrong sides together, and press.

9 With right sides together, aligning the raw edges and matching the cuff seam to the underarm seam, pin and sew the cuffs to the ends of the sleeves. Finish the seam allowances, then press the seam allowances towards the cuffs. Topstitch the seam allowances to the cuffs, using a 3-mm (⅛-in.) stitch length.

10 Measure around your waist, then deduct 2.5 cm (1 in.) for a snug fit. Cut a piece of elastic to this length.

11 To create the waist casing, turn and press the waist edge of the bodice to the wrong side by 1 cm (⅜ in.) and then by a further 3 cm (1¼ in.). Sew the casing (see Special Technique: Fold-down Waist Casing for Elastic, page 197), leaving a 10-cm (4-in.) gap.

12 Insert the elastic into the casing, then overlap the ends by 1 cm (⅜ in.) and zigzag together. Slipstitch or machine stitch the gap closed. Stretch out the elastic to evenly distribute the gathered waist edge. Press the top.

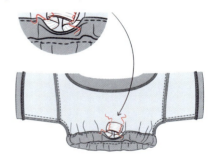

TROUSERS

Prepare the pieces

1 Lay out the pattern pieces as shown in the cutting guide. Cut out and transfer any markings to the fabric (see page 37).

2 Following the manufacturer's instructions, apply interfacing to the wrong side of the front waist facing (see page 35). Finish the raw side edges of the trousers and the curved crotch edges (see page 38).

3 With right sides together, matching the notches, pin the front and back trousers together and sew the inseams. Press the seams open.

4 On the left trouser leg, match the notches on the front and back, then pin the side seam from the hem up to the notches. There should be some excess fabric around the top edge of the back trouser. Find the zip notch on the back trouser edge and insert the invisible zip (see page 155). The zip stop should be below the seam allowance.

5 Pin the rest of the trouser leg together and stitch it closed, stopping at the last stitch of the zip. Press the seam open and turn the leg right side out.

6 With right sides together, matching the inseams, wrap the unfinished right trouser leg around the left trouser leg. Pin and sew the crotch seam, then press the seam open.

7 At the front, top edge of the trousers, fold over the pleat markings away from the centre front seam. Pin the pleats and sew along the pleat fold for about 7 cm (3 in.) to hold them in place. Steam press the pleats away from the centre front.

8 The back portion will be elasticated, so hold a piece of elastic (slightly stretched) across the back of your waistline to check the fit and cut a length that feels comfortable. You will probably need around 35 cm (14 in.), but adjust the length to suit.

9 To create a casing for the elastic, fold and press 1 cm (⅜ in.) to the wrong side around the top edge of the back trouser. Then fold and press 3 cm (1¼ in.) over to the right side.

10 Open the zip. At the zip edge of the back trouser, pin one end of the elastic to the zip seam allowance and zigzag stitch it in place. (Note: You're pinning it to the side of the zip that's nearest the back trouser.)

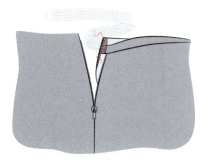

11 Pin the casing over the elastic and sew down the side of the casing, stitching as close as possible to the zip teeth. Turn the casing over to the wrong side of the garment and enclose the elastic within the casing.

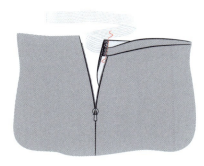

12 Working on the wrong side, stretch the elastic all the way across the back of the trousers and pin it in place. Zigzag stitch the elastic close to the side seam at the back of the trousers.

13 Pin the casing in place and carefully stitch along the bottom folded edge, stretching the elastic as you do so and taking care not to catch the elastic in the stitching.

14 Finish the bottom edge of the front waist facing. With right sides together, pin it to the top edge of the front trouser and sew from one edge to the other, stopping just short of the zip. At the zip side of the front trouser, fold the facing and waistline seam allowances down and pin to the zip tape. Sew the side of the facing to the zip seam allowance, stitching as close as possible to the zip teeth.

15 At the other end of the facing, fold the facing and waistline seam allowances down. Pin and sew from the top to the bottom edge of the facing, as in step 14.

16 With right sides together, sandwich the unstitched back trouser edge between the front trouser and the facing. Pin together and sew from the top edge to the bottom of the trouser. Press the seam open. Turn the facing over to the wrong side of the garment.

17 Finish the bottom of the trouser legs. Fold over 1 cm (⅜ in.) followed by a further 1.5 cm (⅝ in.) to the wrong side and sew the hem.

Patchwork

There's a long history of using scraps and cutting up old, unwearable garments to make new ones. This section shows off the very simplest of patchwork techniques – piecing even-sized squares together to make larger pieces of fabric that you can then transform into stylish clothes and accessories.

Quilted Jacket

Made from co-ordinating denim scraps (although you could, of course, cut the pieces from a single piece of new fabric), this jacket is ever so easy to make – there are only three pattern pieces! Binding around the edges gives a really neat finish.

Materials

- Approx. 100 10-cm (4-in.) co-ordinating squares of fabric for the patchwork
- 1.8 m (2 yd) backing fabric
- 1.2 m (1⅜ yd) fusible wadding (batting)
- Approx. 5 m (5½ yd.) bias binding, 25 mm (1 in.) wide
- Basic sewing kit (see page 32)
- ¼-in. machine foot (optional)
- Walking foot (optional)

Difficulty level

Confident sewer

Fabric suggestions

Leftover: denim, garbadine, needlecord, structured cotton fabrics

Design notes

Use a 1.5-cm (⅝-in.) seam allowance throughout, unless otherwise stated.

You can, of course, make your squares for the patchwork larger or smaller than we did, but whatever size you choose, you'll need enough to create a patchwork piece approx. 100 cm (40 in.) square from which to cut the jacket front and sleeves.

Finished garment measurements	8	10	12	14	16	18	20	22
Bust (cm)	102	107	112	117	122	127	132	137
Bust (in.)	40	42	44	46	48	50	52	54
Sleeve length (cm)	48.5	49	49.5	50	50.5	51	51.5	52
Sleeve length (in.)	19	19¼	19½	19¾	20	20	20¼	20½
Front length (cm)	48.5	49	49.5	50	51	51.5	52	52.5
Front length (in.)	19	19¼	19½	19¾	20	20¼	20½	20¾
Back length (cm)	50.5	51	51.5	52	53	53.5	54	54.5
Back length (in.)	20	20	20¼	20½	21	21	21¼	21½

CUTTING GUIDE

Patchwork

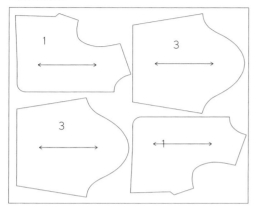

Wadding

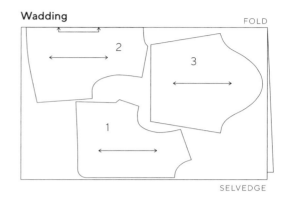

150 cm (60 in.) wide backing

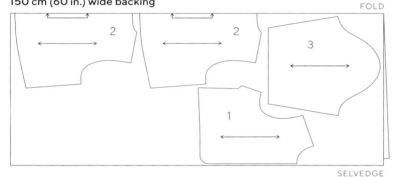

1 Front – cut 1 pair in patchwork, 1 pair in wadding and 1 pair in backing fabric *

2 Back – cut 1 on the fold in wadding and 2 on the fold in backing fabric **

3 Sleeve – cut 1 pair in patchwork, 1 pair in wadding and 1 pair in backing fabric

* Cut the wadding and backing fabric fronts 2.5 cm (1 in.) larger than the patchwork fronts.

** We used the same fabric for both the backing and the back of the jacket, but you could use a different fabric for the back if you prefer.

THE SEWING STARTS HERE

Prepare the pieces

1 Select your patchwork squares and lay them out in your chosen pattern. Consider the colour, pattern and texture placement and bear in mind how you will position your pattern pieces on the patchwork. For each patchwork piece (two fronts and two sleeves), you will need a rectangle measuring four squares across and six squares down – 24 squares for each piece. (You may need a few more if you decide to place your squares on the diagonal.)

2 Stitch the patchwork squares for each rectangle together in six rows of four. Press all the seam allowances to one side – preferably towards the darker fabrics. Press the seam allowances in opposite directions on alternate rows; this lessens the bulk in the seam when you come to stitch the rows together.

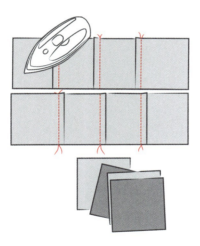

TOP TIPS

◦ You may find it easier and faster to chain piece the squares – in other words, sew them together in pairs without cutting the thread after each pair. Just keep sewing, then feed the next pair of squares under the machine foot.

◦ The seam allowances in patchwork are generally 6 mm (¼ in.) – so if you intend to do a lot of patchwork, it's worth investing in a ¼-in. machine foot to keep the seam allowances consistent.

3 Next, stitch the rows together, nestling the seam allowances together as shown. When you have stitched all six rows for each piece together, press all the seams between the rows to one side, all in the same direction.

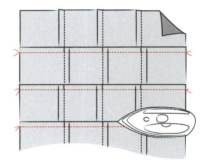

4 Lay out the four patchwork fabrics right side up. Select the area of patchwork you want to feature in your garment and place the pattern pieces on top. Pin and cut out two fronts and two sleeves. Mark the notches and the darts on the front pieces.

TOP TIPS

◦ Remember to flip the patterns before you cut the second one of each piece, so that you cut a left and a right.

◦ When you cut the fronts, make sure that the patchwork seams align across the two pieces.

5 Lay out the wadding (batting) and place the front patchwork pieces on top. Roughly cut out the wadding, cutting 2.5 cm (1 in.) outside the patchwork piece. Mark the dart positions, then cut the darts out of the wadding to reduce bulk.

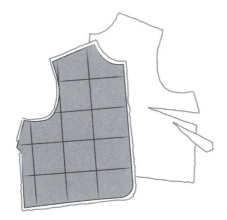

6 Cut the backing pieces for the fronts, again cutting them 2.5 cm (1 in.) larger than the patchwork pieces. You now have a patchwork piece and a slightly larger wadding and backing fabric piece for each jacket front. Mark the position of the darts on the backing fabric pieces, but do not cut them out.

7 Cut a wadding and a backing fabric piece for each sleeve and for the back of the jacket, cutting them the same size as the pattern pieces.

·······································

TOP TIP

Space the lines evenly and keep the distance in proportion with the patchwork squares. For example, you might choose to stitch down the middle of each square and 'in the ditch' between squares.

·······································

8 Place the backing fabric for the front pieces right side down on your work surface, with the wadding on top. Then centre the patchwork fronts right side up on top, so that the wadding is sandwiched in the middle. Make sure all the pieces are flat and that the darts line up. Using a hot, dry iron, press the fronts to adhere the wadding. Then turn the pieces over and press the backing fabric side. Repeat with the jacket back and sleeves.

9 Change the foot of your machine to a walking foot/dual feed foot, if you have one, and set the stitch length slightly longer than normal. Starting from the centre of the front, topstitch a vertical line all the way from the shoulder to the hem through all three layers. Add another vertical line to the right of the first, then another line to the left, spacing the lines evenly. Repeat until you have quilted the entire front. Do not turn the work – only quilt the front pieces, not the sleeves or the back piece.

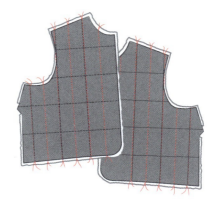

10 Once you have quilted the front, trim off the excess backing fabric and wadding so that they're the same size as the patchwork. Finish the raw edges at the sides, shoulders and armholes.

Sew the jacket

11 Pin and sew the bust darts on the jacket fronts (see page 42), making sure you catch the edge of the cut-out wadding dart in your stitching. Press the darts down, towards the hem.

12 With right sides together, lining up the darts and corresponding notches, pin the fronts to the back at the shoulder and side seams. Stitch in place.

13 On the sleeves, turn the cuff edge to the wrong side by 1.5 cm (⅝ in.) Pin and topstitch in place. With right sides together, stitch the underarm seams.

14 With right sides together lining up the underarm and side seam and matching the notches, pin the sleeves into the armholes (see page 43). Stitch in place. Where the underarm and side seams meet, push the seam allowances in opposite directions so that they sit neatly next to each other to reduce bulk.

Bind the edges

15 Open out your bias binding. With the jacket right side out, lining up the raw edge of the binding with the outer edge of the jacket, lay the end of the binding at the bottom of the centre back, overlapping the centre point by 6 mm (¼ in.). Pin the binding in place along bottom, centre front edges and neckline of the jacket. Starting 5 cm (2 in.) from the centre back point, sew the binding in place, mitring the corners and overlapping the ends (see Special Technique: Attaching Binding, opposite).

SPECIAL TECHNIQUE: ATTACHING BINDING

You can either use ready-made bias binding or make your own.

1 Unfold one long edge and place it with right sides together along the edge you plan to bind. Pin and then stitch it in place along the crease line. Trim the seam to 6 mm (¼ in).

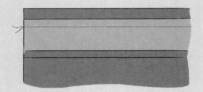

2 **Revealed method**
To use bias binding as a trim, fold the bias binding over the seam allowance to the wrong side and pin and tack (baste) in place. Topstitch from the right side (see page 40), then remove the tacking stitches.

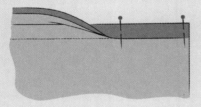

3 **Concealed method**
With this method, the binding is visible only on the inside of the bound edge. It is suitable for necklines and armholes and functions as a mini facing (see page 44). Trim the seam allowance, then fold the whole width of the bias binding to the wrong side. The stitch line joining the bias binding to the main piece will lie exactly on the edge of the garment when it is finished. Topstitch in place..

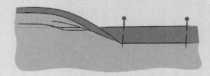

Overlapping the ends

If the binding ends will meet, as they will at the centre back of the quilted patchwork jacket, the ends will need to be overlapped as inconspicuously as possible.

Before you start pinning the binding to the garment, turn the raw end of the start of the binding to the wrong side and press. Pin this end to the garment, and follow step 1, above. When you reach the end, allow the un-neatened end of the binding to overlap the turned start by about 1 cm (⅜ in.) and stitch it down. When you fold the binding over to the wrong side of the garment in step 5, the neatened end will be uppermost.

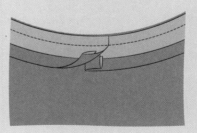

ACCESSORY

Tote

Small pieces of brightly coloured African wax fabrics give this bag a really vibrant feel. The handy patch pockets provide invaluable extra storage; edge them in a toning plain fabric so that they stand out.

Materials

- Woven fabric scraps amounting to roughly 1 m (1 yd)
- 50 cm (20 in.) lining fabric
- 50 cm (20 in.) plain fabric (matching or contrasting) for the pockets
- 50 cm (20 in.) medium-weight interfacing
- Basic sewing kit (see page 32)

Difficulty level

Confident beginner

Fabric suggestions

Quilting cotton, African wax fabrics, denim

Design notes

Use a 1.5-cm (⅝-in.) seam allowance throughout, unless otherwise stated.

Finished size

45.5 x 35 cm (18 x 13¾ in.)

CUTTING GUIDE

1 Bag – cut 2 in patchwork fabric, 2 in lining fabric and 4 in interfacing, each measuring 48.5 x 38 cm (19 x 15 in.)

2 Patch pockets – cut 2 in patchwork fabric, each measuring 26.5 x 18.5 cm (10½ x 7¼ in.)

3 Pocket side panels – cut 2 in plain fabric, each measuring 26.5 x 5.5 cm (10½ x 2¼ in.)

4 Pocket top panels – cut 2 in plain fabric, each measuring 10 x 21 cm (4 x 8¼ in.)

5 Straps – cut 2 in patchwork fabric, each measuring 65 x 11.5 cm (25½ x 4½ in.)

THE SEWING STARTS HERE

Prepare the pieces

1 Neaten the fabric scraps into 10-cm (4-in.) squares. Pin them right sides together. Using a 1-cm (⅜-in.) seam allowance, sew scraps together until you have created a larger fabric piece. Ensure you maintain the grain lines so that the fabric doesn't stretch out of shape. Press the seams open.

2 Using the dimensions specified in the cutting guide, cut out the pieces you need. Use the patchwork fabric for the outer bag, patch pockets and straps, lining fabric for the lining, and plain fabric for the pocket top and side panels.

3 Following the manufacturer's instructions, apply interfacing to the wrong side of the outer and lining bag pieces (see page 35).

Prepare the patch pockets

Side panels add structure and body to the patch pockets.

4 With right sides together, pin the pocket side panel to the edge of the patch pocket that will sit at the middle of the bag front. Sew together and finish the raw edge. Press the seam open.

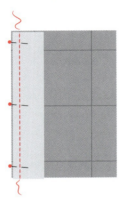

5 With wrong sides together, fold the pocket top panel in half lengthways. Aligning the raw edges, pin it to the wrong side of the pocket's top edge. Sew together and trim the seam allowance.

6 Press the seam allowances up. Fold the top panel along the seam line and press it over to the right side of the pocket.

7 Fold the side panel to the wrong side along the seam line and press.

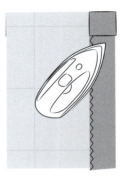

8 Topstitch from the top to the bottom of this side of the pocket.

9 Fold and press the finished raw edge of the side panel under by 1.5 cm (⅝ in.). Place the patch pocket at the lower edge of the outer bag front, with the wrong side of the pocket against the right side of the bag. Stitch from the top to the bottom of the side panel, as close to the fold as possible, to attach the side panel to the bag front. The side panel now forms a narrow gusset that adds depth to the pocket so that you can slide items into it more easily.

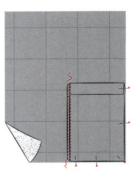

You will be left with two raw edges on the patch pocket at this point – the bottom edge and the edge that will sit at the bag's side seam. Repeat steps 4–8 with the other patch pocket and pocket top and side panels.

10 Pin the two outer bag pieces right sides together, making sure that the pocket edges are securely pinned as well. Stitch around the side and bottom edges of the bag, leaving the top edge open. Press the seams open.

11 Fold the strap in half lengthways, wrong sides together, and press. Then open the strap out, turn the long raw edges to the wrong side by 1.5 cm (⅝ in.) and press. Fold the strap in half down the centre crease line again and topstitch along each long side as close as possible to the edge.

12 With the outer bag right side out, pin the straps to the top edge, 10 cm (4 in.) away from the side seams, and tack (baste) in place.

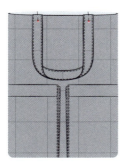

13 Pin the two lining bag pieces right sides together and sew the side seams and bottom edge, leaving a 10-cm (4-in.) gap in the bottom for turning out the main bag fabric through. Press the seams open.

14 Before you stitch the outer bag and lining together, you will need to create a box corner base. With the outer bag wrong side out, pinch the bottom corner so that the side seam lies directly over the base seam, forming a triangle. Pin in place. Mark a point 5 cm (2 in.) from the tip of the triangle and sew along that line. Trim off the excess fabric and press to set the stitches. Repeat with the other bottom corners of the outer bag and the bag lining.

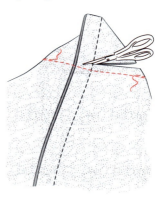

TOP TIP

When you form the corner triangles, make sure that the seam allowances on the side and base of the bag face in opposite directions, so that they 'nest' neatly together; this also reduces the bulk.

15 With right sides together, matching the side seams and top edges, tuck the outer bag inside the lining, sandwiching the straps in between. Pin and sew around the top edge.

16 Carefully pull the outer bag through the gap in the lining. Close the gap by sewing as close as possible to the folded edge at the bottom of the lining fabric

17 With the bag straps out of the way, carefully topstitch around the top edge of the bag.

Bum Bag

If you haven't got enough scraps left to make a whole garment, why not scale things down and make small accessories such as this bum bag!

Materials

- 50 cm (20 in.) main fabric
- 50 cm (20 in.) lining fabric
- 50 cm (20 in.) medium-weight iron-on interfacing
- 25-cm (10-in.) closed-end zip
- 1 m (1 yd) webbing straps, 2.5 cm (1 in.) wide
- 2.5-cm (1-in.) clip buckle
- Basic sewing kit (see page 32)

Difficulty level

Confident beginner

Fabric suggestions

Leftovers from projects using mid- to heavy-weight fabrics

Design notes

Use a 1.5-cm (⅝-in.) seam allowance throughout, unless otherwise stated.

Finished size

34.5 x 29 cm (13½ x 11½ in.)

CUTTING GUIDE

1 Top panel – cut 1 main fabric, 1 in lining fabric and 1 in interfacing, all on the fold

2 Front panel – cut 1 in main fabric, 1 in lining fabric and 1 in interfacing, all on the fold

3 Back panel – cut 1 in main fabric, 1 in lining fabric and 1 in interfacing, all on the fold

4 Side tabs – cut 4 in main fabric

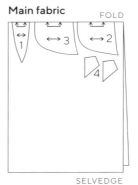

Main fabric

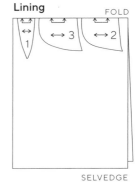

Lining

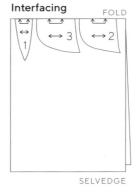

Interfacing

THE SEWING STARTS HERE

Prepare the pieces

1 You can make this bag using either plain or patchworked fabric. If you choose the patchwork option, you will need to create three patchworked fabrics, each measuring approx. 25 x 35 cm (10 x 14 in.). Cut 10-cm (4-in.) squares of your chosen fabrics and stitch them together, following the instructions for the Quilted Jacket on page 176.

2 Lay out the pattern pieces as shown in the cutting guide. Cut out and transfer the zip markings to the wrong side of the main and lining fabric front panels (see page 37).

3 Following the manufacturer's instructions, apply interfacing to the wrong side of all the main fabric panels (see page 35).

Insert the zip

4 With right sides together, pin the main and lining fabric front panels together.

5 Sew around the marked-out zip guide to create a long, narrow rectangle. Cut along the guideline in the middle of the rectangle and then snip from the end of the guideline into each corner of the rectangle, cutting as close as possible to the corners but without snipping through the stitches.

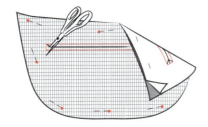

6 Remove the pins. Pass the lining through the hole in the rectangle, then press to keep the lining in place.

7 Pin the front and lining panels together again to keep the layers flat while you stitch the zip. Pin the zip behind the cut-out rectangle, right side up, so that the zip teeth are visible through the hole. Using a zipper foot, carefully topstitch around the hole to secure the zip in place. Open the zip.

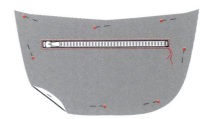

Assemble the bag

8 To create the outer shell, gather the following main fabric pieces: top panel, front panel and back panel. With right sides together, pin one edge of the top panel to the top edge of the front panel, avoiding the lining fabric. Then pin the other side of the top panel to the top edge of the back panel, again right sides together. Stitch them together and press the seams open. The three main fabric panels of the bag are now stitched together in one piece, with the top panel in the middle.

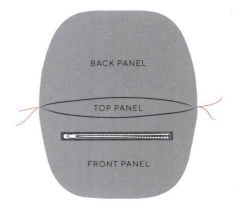

Attach the straps

9 Measure around your waist and add 15 cm (6 in.). Cut two straps of webbing to this length for the straps. Following the manufacturer's instructions, attach the buckle to one end of one strap and the slider to one end of the other strap.

10 With right sides together, pin one end of the bag strap to the short straight edge of the side tab.

11 Pin another side tab right side down on top, sandwiching the strap in between. Sew around three sides of the tab, as shown.

12 Slip the corners, turn right side out and press. Repeat steps 10–12 with the other tabs and strap.

13 Pin the tabs to the right side of the front panel, then fold the back panel over the front, right sides together and aligning the raw edges. Pin all around and stitch through all layers, avoiding the straps and the front panel's lining. Trim the seam allowances and clip the curves (see page 39).

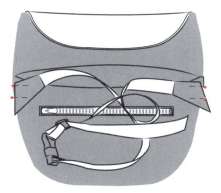

14 Now pin the top lining panel to the front and back lining panels, so that it sits in between them, just as you did with the main fabric panels in step 8. Stitch them together and press the seams open.

15 Fold the back lining panel over the front, just as you did with the outer bag pieces in step 13, and sew them together, leaving a 10-cm (4-in.) gap. Trim the seam allowance and clip the curves around the lining fabric, but not around the gap.

16 Pull the main fabric bag through the gap to the right side. Hand or machine stitch the gap in the lining closed, then press the bag.

Sleep Wear

Whether you want silky PJs or cosy brushed cotton loungewear for those winter 'duvet days' when all you want to do is curl up on the sofa and binge watch box sets of your favourite shows, the designs in this section are just the ticket.

VERSION 1

Women's Pyjamas

An Oriental-style patterned satin makes these short-sleeved PJs look really luxurious. You could shorten the legs to make shorts, if you prefer.

Materials

For the top:

- Sizes 8–14: 80 cm (1 yd) fabric, 150 cm (60 in.) wide
  Sizes 16–22: 1.4 m (1⅝ yd) fabric, 150 cm (60 in.) wide
- 80 cm (32 in.) interfacing
- 5 buttons, 1 cm (⅜ in.) in diameter

For the trousers:

- Sizes 8–14: 2 m (2¼ yd) fabric, 150 cm (60 in.) wide
  Sizes 16–22: 2.2 m (2½ yd) fabric, 150 cm (60 in.) wide
- Approx. 2 m (2¼yd) elastic, 2.5 cm (1 in.) wide

For both items:

- Basic sewing kit (see page 32)

Difficulty level

Intermediate

Fabric suggestions

Satin, silk, cotton poplin

Design notes

Use a 1.5-cm (⅝-in.) seam allowance throughout, unless otherwise stated.

Finished garment
measurements

TOP	8	10	12	14	16	18	20	22
Bust (cm)	98	103	108	113	118	123	128	133
Bust (in.)	38½	40½	42½	44½	46½	48½	50½	52½
Sleeve length (cm)	27	27.5	28	28.5	29	29.5	30	30.5
Sleeve length (in.)	10½	10¾	11	11¼	11½	11¾	12	12
Front length (cm)	48.5	49	49.5	50	51	51.5	52	52.5
Front length (in.)	19	19¼	19½	19¾	20	20¼	20½	20¾
Back length (cm)	69.5	70	70.5	71	72	72.5	73	73.5
Back length (in.)	27¼	27½	27¾	28	28¼	28½	28¾	29

TROUSERS								
Waist (cm)	92.5	97.5	102.5	107.5	112.5	117.5	122.5	127.5
Waist (in.)	36½	38½	40½	42½	44¼	46¼	48¼	50¼
Hip (cm)	100	105	110	115	120	125	130	135
Hip (in.)	39½	41½	43¼	45¼	47¼	49¼	51¼	53¼
Inside leg (cm)	79	79	79	79	79	79	79	79
Inside leg (in.)	31	31	31	31	31	31	31	31

CUTTING GUIDE

Sizes 8–14: 150 cm (60 in.) wide fabric

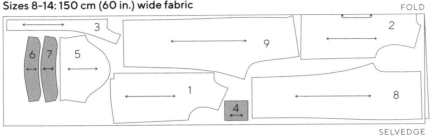

Sizes 16–22: 150 cm (60 in.) wide fabric

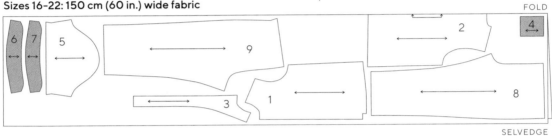

1 Front – cut 1 pair

2 Back – cut 1 on the fold

3 Front facing – cut 1 pair in fabric and 1 pair in interfacing

4 Pocket – cut 1

5 Sleeve – cut 1 pair

6 Top collar – cut 1 in fabric and 1 in interfacing

7 Under collar – cut 1 in fabric and 1 in interfacing

8 Front trouser – cut 1 pair

9 Back trouser – cut 1 pair

10 Elastic template – do not cut

Interfacing

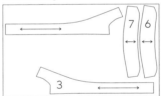

SPECIAL TECHNIQUE: FOLD-DOWN WAIST CASING FOR ELASTIC

A fold-down casing is made by turning down the waist edge of the garment to form a channel into which elastic or a drawstring is inserted. It is best used on straight edges.

1 Around the waistline, turn under the amount specified on the pattern.

2 Machine stitch along the lower edge of the casing, leaving a gap at the centre back seam for the elastic. Work a second row of stitching all the way around the top edge.

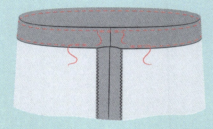

3 Attach a safety pin to one end of the elastic and feed it through the casing, making sure the other end doesn't disappear inside the casing by pinning it to the garment at the start of the gap. Ease the waistline fabric along as you feed the elastic through, then pin the two ends of elastic together.

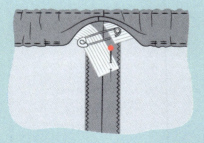

4 Stitch the ends of the elastic together by stitching around them in a square shape without lifting the needle; this is known as box stitching. Alternatively, zigzag stitch the ends together. Ease the elastic back into the casing.

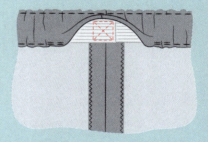

5 Slipstitch or machine stitch the gap in the bottom edge of the casing closed.

TOP

Prepare the pieces

1 Lay out the pattern pieces as shown in the cutting guide. Cut out and transfer any markings to the fabric (see page 37), including the pocket, buttonhole and button placements.

2 Following the manufacturer's instructions, apply interfacing to the wrong side of the front facings and top and under collar pieces (see page 35).

3 Stay stitch (see page 40) the neckline edges of the front facings and the front and back pyjama necklines 1 cm (⅜ in.) from the raw edge.

Sew the pocket

4 Along the top edge of the pocket, fold 1 cm (⅜ in.) to the wrong side and press. Then turn it under again by 2 cm (¾ in.) and stitch close to the fold line. Turn under the remaining raw edges by 1.5 cm (⅝ in.) and press.

5 Following the markings on the pattern, pin the pocket to the left-hand side of the pyjama front. Stitch in place close to the side and bottom edges.

Assemble the pyjama top

6 With right sides together, pin and sew the front and back pieces together at the shoulders. Finish the seam allowances (see page 38) and press the seams open.

7 With right sides together, matching the notches, pin the top collar to the under collar. Stitch along the two short sides and the long side with the centre back notch, leaving the edge with multiple notches open. Trim the seam allowances and snip into the corners. Turn the collar right side out and press.

8 To make the stitching process easier, snip into the curved neckline of the pyjama top up to (but not through!) the stay stitching.

9 On the right side, matching the notches, pin the open edge of the under collar to the neck edge of the pyjama top. Match the centre back, shoulder seams and the diagonal 'fold line' notches; the 'fold line' notch is marked as a cross on the pattern.

10 Clip into the seam allowance at the shoulder seam notches on the top collar, then fold the open edge of the top collar under between the notches. (This section will be used later to conceal the raw edge of the back neckline.)

11 Tack (baste) the collar to the pyjama neckline from one front neck edge to the other. Do not stitch the back neckline section of the top collar.

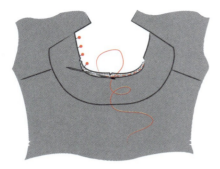

12 The front portion of the neckline will be finished using the front facings. First, finish the unnotched, curved edge and the shoulder edge of each interfaced facing. Clip into the seam allowance of the neckline of the facings up to the stay stitching.

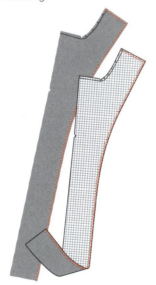

13 With right sides together, pin the facings to the neck edge of the pyjama fronts all the way down the centre fronts. Stitch the front from one hem to the other, turning at the corners and avoiding catching the free edges of the collar and the back neckline section of the top collar in the stitching. Trim the seam allowances and the corners and snip into the curved seam allowance.

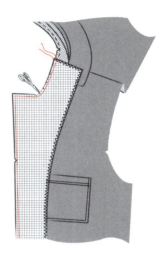

14 Turn the facings to the wrong side of the garment and the back neckline seam allowance in towards the collar. Press.

15 Pin the folded-under edge of the top collar over the back neckline seam. Stitch 'in the ditch' (see page 40) along the back neckline seam to secure the top collar.

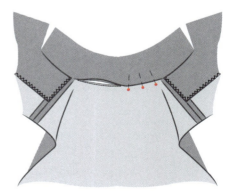

16 At this point, the only unstitched section should be the shoulder edge of the front facing. To keep it in place, tack it to the shoulder seam allowance on both sides of the pyjama front.

17 Press the collar and fold over the top collar and the front facing at the diagonal fold line.

Sew the sleeves

18 Finish the seam allowances of the armholes and sleeves all the way around, except for the sleeve hems. With right sides together, matching the shoulder seams and armhole notches, pin and sew the sleeves into the armholes (see page 43). Press the seams open.

19 Fold the top in half, right sides together, matching the underarm and side edges of the back and front. Pin and stitch the underarm and side seams from the sleeve to the hem of the pyjama top. Press the seams open.

20 At the ends of the sleeves, fold 1 cm (⅜ in.) to the wrong side and press. Then fold it a further 2.5 cm (1 in.) and press again. Pin in place and topstitch close to the inner fold.

Hem the top

21 Turn the bottom edge of the facings to the right side of the garment and pin to the bottom edge of the pyjama. Stitch across to the end of the facing, trim the seam allowance. Turn the facing back to the wrong side of the garment and press.

22 Around the hem, turn 1.5 cm (⅝ in.) to the wrong side and press, followed by a further 2.5 cm (1 in.). Pin in place. Starting from the centre front, topstitch the hem close to the fold.

Stitch the buttons and buttonholes

23 Following the pattern for the placement, work the buttonholes (see page 48) on the right front. Overlap the buttonhole side over the button side and mark the button positions through the buttonholes. Stitch the buttons in place.

TROUSERS

1 Finish the raw edges of the inseam and side edges of the trouser legs.

2 Pin a front and a back trouser leg together right sides together, matching the notches. Stitch them together along the inseam and side seam. Press the seams open. Repeat with the other front and back legs.

3 With right sides together, matching the notches and inseams, insert one trouser leg into the other. Pin and sew them together around the crotch curve. Finish the raw edges and press the seam open. Turn right side out.

4 Using the elastic template that comes with the pattern, cut the right length of elastic for your size.

5 At the waist edge turn 1.5 cm (⅝ in.) and then a further 3 cm (1¼ in.) to the wrong side and press to create a casing. Pin in place. Stitch the casing and insert the elastic (see Special Technique: Fold-down Waist Casing for Elastic, page 197).

6 At the bottom of the legs, turn 1 cm (⅜ in.) and then a further 4 cm (1½ in.) to the wrong side and press. Pin in place and sew close to the fold.

ACCESSORY

Sleeping Mask

Use scraps left over from the main project to make a matching sleeping mask.

Materials

- Fat quarter of your chosen fabric
- 25 cm (10 in.) wadding (batting)
- Approx. 35 cm (14 in.) elastic, 1 cm (⅜ in.) wide
- Basic sewing kit (see page 32)
- Turning tool

Difficulty level

Beginner

Fabric suggestions

Leftovers from cotton, satin and silk projects

Design notes

Use a 1.5-cm (⅝-in.) seam allowance throughout, unless otherwise stated.

Finished size

22 x 10.5 cm (8¾ x 4 in.)

CUTTING GUIDE

1 Mask – cut 2 in fabric and 1 in wadding
2 Strap – cut 1 in fabric

THE SEWING STARTS HERE

1 Cut out the pattern pieces and transfer any markings to the fabric (see page 37).

2 With right sides together, fold the strap in half lengthways and pin in place. Using a 1-cm (⅜-in.) seam allowance, sew along the long edge. Trim the seam allowances and turn the strap right side out.

3 Stretch the elastic around the back of your head, from one ear to the other, and work out what's a comfortable length – not so tight that it hurts your head but not so loose that the mask can slip off when worn. Cut the elastic to this length. Attach a safety pin to one end of the elastic, then feed the elastic through the tube. Pin the elastic to the raw edges of the strap at both ends.

4 Align the strap ends with the notches on either side of what will be the right side of the mask. Pin in place. With right sides together, lay the other mask piece on top, sandwiching the strap between the two main fabric pieces. Place the wadding on top and pin all layers together.

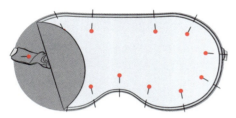

5 Stitch all around through all layers, leaving a 5-cm (2-in.) gap along the top edge of the mask. Trim and clip the seam allowance (see page 39) and turn the mask right side out through the gap.

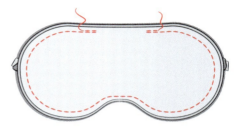

6 Turn under the edges of the gap, pin together, and slipstitch the gap closed. You may also wish to topstitch all the way around the edge of the mask.

VERSION 2

Men's Pyjamas

The sleeves are full length and the shape of the collar differs slightly from the Women's Pyjamas on page 194, but otherwise the construction method is exactly the same.

Materials

For the top:

- 1.6 m (1¾ yd) fabric, 150 cm (60 in.) wide
- 80 cm (1 yd) interfacing
- 7 buttons, 1 cm (⅜ in.) in diameter

For the trousers:

- 2.2 m (2½ yd) fabric, 150 cm (60 in.) wide
- Approx. 2 m (2¼ yd) elastic, 2.5 cm (1 in.) wide (depending on the waist size)

For both items:

- Basic sewing kit (see page 32)

Difficulty level

Intermediate

Fabric suggestions

Cotton shirting, polycotton, cotton poplin

Design notes

Use a 1.5-cm (⅝-in.) seam allowance throughout, unless otherwise stated.

150 cm (60 in.) wide fabric

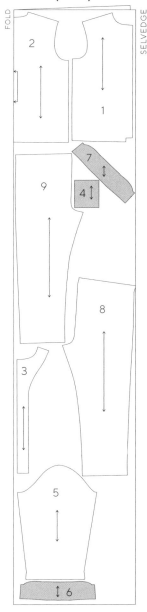

Interfacing

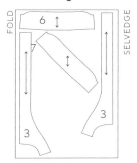

CUTTING GUIDE

1. Front – cut 1 pair
2. Back – cut 1 on the fold
3. Front facing – cut 1 pair in fabric and 1 pair in interfacing
4. Pocket – cut 1
5. Sleeve – cut 1 pair
6. Top collar – cut 1 in fabric and 1 in interfacing
7. Under collar – cut 1 in fabric and 1 in interfacing
8. Front trouser – cut 1 pair
9. Back trouser – cut 1 pair
10. Elastic template – do not cut

Finished garment measurements

TOP	S	M	L	XL	XXL
Chest (cm)	110	115	120	125	130
Chest (in.)	43¼	45¼	47¼	49¼	51¼
Sleeve length (cm)	59.5	60	60.5	61	61.5
Sleeve length (in.)	23½	23¾	24	24	24¼
Front length (cm)	73.5	74	74.5	75	76
Front length (in.)	29	29	29¼	29½	30
Back length (cm)	71	71.5	72	72.5	73
Back length (in.)	28	28¼	28½	28½	28¾

TROUSERS	S	M	L	XL	XXL
Waist (cm)	73	78	83	88	93
Waist (in.)	28¾	30¾	32¾	34¾	36¾
Inside leg (cm)	77	77	77	77	77
Inside leg (in.)	30¼	30¼	30¼	30¼	30¼

THE SEWING STARTS HERE

Top

Make the top in the same way as for the Women's Pyjamas (page 199), with the following changes:

- Step 4: Along the top edge of the pocket, fold the fabric to the wrong side by 1 cm (⅜ in.) and then by a further 2.5 cm (1 in.) and press.

- Step 5: Stitch the pocket to the left front.

- Step 9: When you pin the under collar to the neck edge, make sure you match the centre back, shoulder seam and front neckline notches.

- Step 20: At the ends of the sleeves, turn 1 cm (⅜ in.) and then a further 4 cm (1½ in.) to the wrong side and press.

- Step 23: Position the buttonholes on the left front and the buttons on the right.

Trousers

Make the trousers in the same way as for the Women's Pyjamas (page 201), with the following changes:

- Step 4: When you create the waist casing, turn the waist edge to the wrong side by 1 cm (⅜ in.) and then by a further 3 cm (1¼ in.). Measure elastic to fit comfortably around the waist, add 2.5 cm (1 in.) and cut. Insert the elastic into the casing (see Special Technique: Fold-down Waist Casing for Elastic, page 197.

Shell Tops

Shell tops – normally short sleeveless tops with button fastenings down the back and a simple shape – are a staple that everyone needs in their wardrobe. Designed to complement a more interesting piece, such as a skirt or trousers, they're often made in plain colours so that the main garment can standout. Here are some ways to ring the changes.

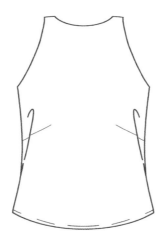

Classic Shell Top

This classic shell top, made in an easy-to-work-with viscose crepe, is a great beginners project.

Materials

- 1 m (1⅛ yd) fabric, 150 cm (60 in.) wide
- 40 cm (16 in.) interfacing
- 1 button, approx. 1 cm (⅜ in.) in diameter
- Basic sewing kit (see page 32)

Difficulty level

Confident beginner

Fabric suggestions

Viscose, cotton gauze, linen, cotton poplin

Design notes

Use a 1.5-cm (⅝-in.) seam allowance throughout, unless otherwise stated.

Finished garment measurements	8	10	12	14	16	18	20	22
Bust (cm)	87.5	92.5	97.5	102.5	107.5	112.5	117.5	122.5
Bust (in.)	34½	36½	38½	40½	42½	44½	46½	48½
Front length (cm)	57	57.5	58	58.5	59	60	60.5	61
Front length (in.)	22½	22¾	23	23	23¼	23½	24¾	24
Back length (cm)	53.5	54	54.5	55	55.5	56.5	57	57.5
Back length (in.)	21	21¼	21½	21¾	22	22¼	22½	22¾

CUTTING GUIDE

150 cm (60 in.) wide fabric

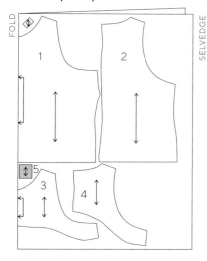

Interfacing

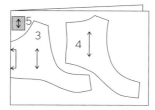

1 Front – cut 1 on the fold

2 Back – cut 1 pair

3 Front facing – cut 1 on the fold in fabric and 1 on the fold in interfacing

4 Back facing – cut 1 pair in fabric and 1 pair in interfacing

5 Buttonhole tab – cut 1 in fabric and 1 in interfacing

THE SEWING STARTS HERE

Prepare the pieces

1 Lay out the pattern pieces as shown in the cutting guide. Cut out and transfer any markings to the fabric (see page 37).

2 Following the manufacturer's instructions, apply interfacing to the wrong side of the front and back facings and the buttonhole tab (see page 35). Finish the raw edges of the shoulders, sides and centre backs.

Sew the darts

3 Pin and sew the front bust darts (see page 42). Press the darts down towards the hem.

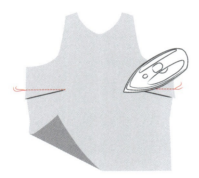

Join the front and back

4 Pin the front and back pieces right sides together and sew along the shoulder seams. Press the seams open. Repeat with the front and back facing pieces. Neaten the lower edge of the facing with a zigzag or edge stitch or on an overlocker (serger).

Attach the facing

5 Attach the facing to the garment (see page 44, steps 2–7).

Sew the buttonhole tab and centre back

6 Fold the buttonhole tab in half widthways and stitch along the two long edges. Turn the tab right side out and press.

7 Place the buttonhole tab on the right side of the left back piece, making sure it sits right up at the neckline. Tack (baste) in place.

8 Bring the left back facing over the buttonhole tab, pin in place and stitch all the way to the end of the facing. Repeat on the other back piece, which doesn't have a buttonhole tab. Snip the centre back neck edge corners and turn the facing through. Press the opening on both back pieces.

9 Place the back pieces right sides together and pin from the hem up to about 1 cm (⅜ in.) past where you sewed the facing to the opening, moving the facing up and out of the way. Stitch in place, then press the centre back seam open.

Finishing touches

10 Around the hem, press 1 cm (⅜ in.) followed by a further 1 cm (⅜ in.) to the wrong side. Pin in place, then stitch all around the hem. Press the hem.

11 Work a buttonhole (see page 48) on the buttonhole tab, then stitch a button to the right back piece to correspond.

VERSION 2

Sleeveless Shell Top

Here, the bodice is split into three sections, creating a triangular shape that makes the garment feel more fitted. The faux 'collar' is actually a facing that's folded over to the front of the garment, so it's not difficult to make.

Materials

- Sizes 8–14: 1.2 m (1⅜ yd) fabric, 150 cm (60 in.) wide
  Sizes 16–22: 1.4 m (1⅝ yd) fabric, 150 cm (60 in.) wide

- 40 cm (16 in.) interfacing

- 2.5 m (2¾ yd) single-fold bias binding, 1.2 cm (½ in.) wide

- Basic sewing kit (see page 32)

Difficulty level

Confident sewer

Fabric suggestions

Viscose, challis, crepe de chine, viscose crepe, voile, crepe backed satin

Design notes

Use a 1.5-cm (⅝-in.) seam allowance throughout, unless otherwise stated.

CUTTING GUIDE

1 Centre front – cut 1

2 Side front – cut 1 pair

3 Back – cut 1 on the fold

4 Front neck facing – cut 1 pair in fabric and 1 pair in interfacing

5 Back neck facing – cut 1 on the fold in fabric and 1 on the fold in interfacing

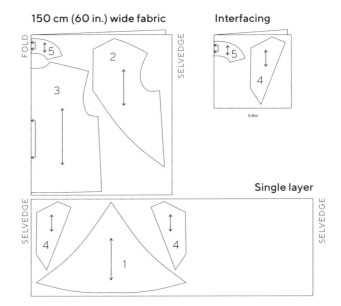

Finished garment measurements	8	10	12	14	16	18	20	22
Bust (cm)	96	101	106	111	116	121	126	131
Bust (in.)	37¾	39¾	41¾	43¾	45¾	47¾	49¾	51¾
Front length (cm)	65.5	66	66.5	67	68	68.5	69	69.5
Front length (in.)	25¾	26	26¼	26½	26¾	27	27¼	27½
Back length (cm)	59	60	60.5	61	61.5	62	62.5	63.5
Back length (in.)	23¼	23½	23¾	24	24¼	24½	24¾	25

THE SEWING STARTS HERE

Prepare the pieces

1 Lay out the pattern pieces as shown in the cutting guide. Cut out and transfer any markings to the fabric (see page 37).

2 Following the manufacturer's instructions, apply interfacing to the wrong side of the front and back neck facings (see page 35).

3 Stay stitch (see page 40) the necklines and armholes. Finish (see page 38) the raw edges of the centre and side front bodice panels.

Assemble the bodice

4 From the pointed corner at the top of the centre front bodice, on the wrong side of the fabric, mark a 1-cm (⅜-in.) seam allowance down each side as far as the notches. Mark the point at which the seam allowances meet below the pointed top corner, too.

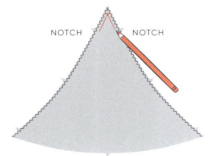

NOTCH   NOTCH

5 With right sides together and notches matching, pin the side front bodice panels to the centre front. Sew from the hem up to the point below the top corner that you marked in step 4 and backstitch. Press the seam open. Repeat on the other side. Fold and lightly press the unstitched flap out of the way.

6 With the unstitched 'centre front' flaps out of the way, pin the left and right side bodice panels together at the centre front and stitch up from point marked in step 4 for only 2 cm (¾ in.), then backstitch. Snip into the notches at the centre front bodice and press the seam allowances towards the side seams to reduce bulk when the facing is inserted. Press the rest of the seam open.

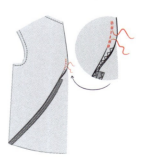

7 With right sides together, matching the notches, pin and sew the front and back bodices together at the shoulder seams. Finish the seam allowances and press the seams open.

Attach the facing

8 With right sides together, pin and sew the interfaced facings together at the shoulder seams. Press the seams open. Neaten the bottom edge of the facing. At the pointed edge of both front facings, fold 1.5 cm (⅝ in.) to the wrong side and press.

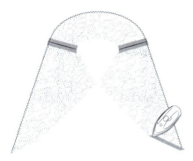

9 With right sides together, matching the notches, pin the facing around the neckline. Sew from the folded corner on the left front facing all the way around to the right front facing, pivoting at the corners for a clean finish and making sure that the seam allowances from step 6 don't get caught in the stitching. Trim the corners and snip into the curves.

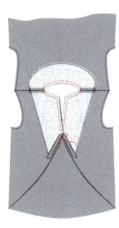

10 Carefully understitch (see page 40) the facing of the back neckline only; the front facing will be visible on the front bodice.

11 Turn the facing over to the right side of the garment and press along the diagonal seam lines of the side bodice pieces to form a collar. Press in place.

12 Secure the facing in place by stitching 'in the ditch' (see page 40) along the shoulder seams. Also stitch the folded-over pointed edge of the front facings (step 8) to the centre front seam allowances on both sides.

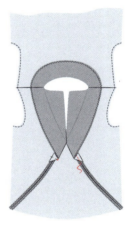

Finish the armholes and side seams

13 Unfold one edge of the bias binding and pin it around the armhole. Stitching along the crease line, sew around the armhole. Snip into the curve, fold the binding to the wrong side and press. Pin the binding in place.

14 Finish the raw edges of the front and back bodice side seams. With right sides together, pin and sew the bodice side seams from the bias tape edge to the hem. Finish and press the seams open.

15 Edge stitch close to the edge of the binding to finish off the armholes.

16 Around the hem, turn 6 mm (¼ in.) and then a further 2 cm (¾ in.) to the wrong side. Pin in place, then stitch all around. Press the hem.

Long-sleeved Shell Top

Based on the same pattern as the Sleeveless Shell Top (page 215), this version has long, puff sleeves and is made in a small-patterned viscose challis, which makes it feel more formal.

Materials

- Sizes 8–14: 1.8 m (2 yd) fabric, 150 cm (60 in.) wide
  Sizes 16–22: 2 m (2¼ yd) fabric, 150 cm (60 in.) wide
- 40 cm (16 in.) interfacing
- 50 cm (20 in.) elastic, 1.2 cm (½ in.) wide
- Basic sewing kit (see page 32)

Difficulty level

Confident sewer

Fabric suggestions

Viscose, challis, crepe de chine, viscose crepe, voile, crepe backed satin

Design notes

Use a 1.5-cm (⅝-in.) seam allowance throughout, unless otherwise stated.

CUTTING GUIDE

1 Centre front – cut 1
2 Side front – cut 1 pair
3 Back – cut 1 on the fold
4 Sleeve – cut 1 pair
5 Front neck facing – cut 1 pair in fabric and 1 pair in interfacing
6 Back neck facing – cut 1 on the fold in fabric and 1 on the fold in interfacing

150 cm (60 in.) wide fabric

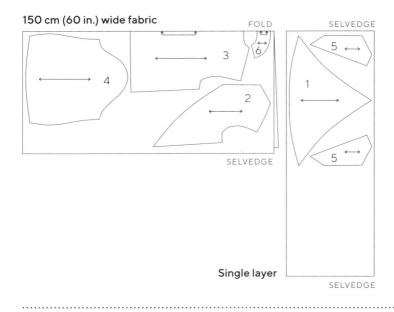

Interfacing

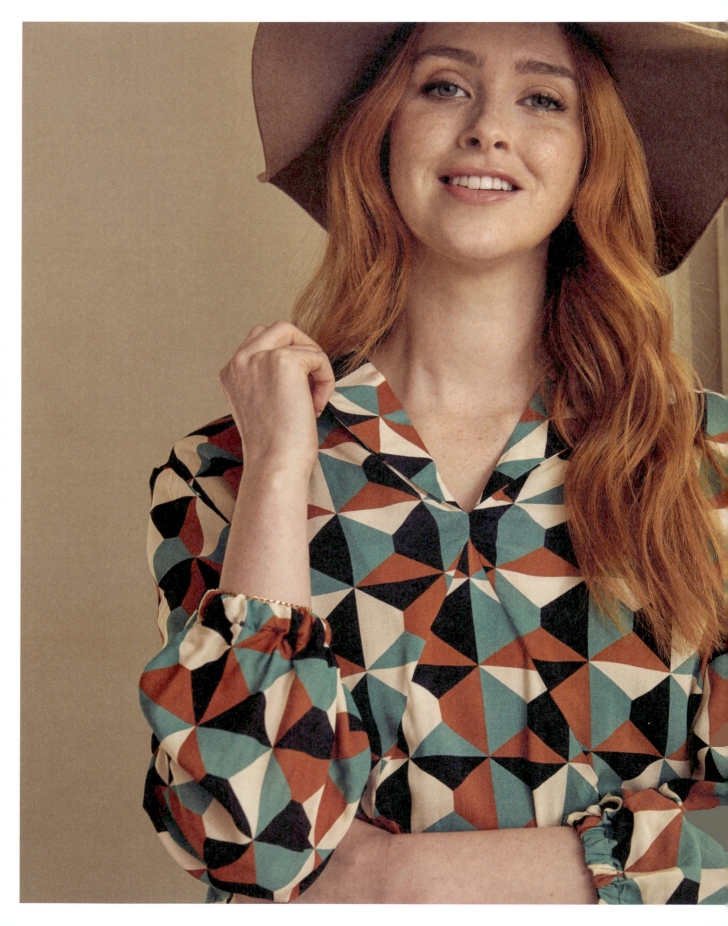

Finished garment measurements	8	10	12	14	16	18	20	22
Bust (cm)	96	101	106	111	116	121	126	131
Bust (in.)	37¾	39¾	41¾	43¾	45¾	47¾	49¾	51¾
Sleeve length (cm)	54.5	55	55.5	56	56.5	57	57.5	58
Sleeve length (in.)	21½	21¾	21¾	22	22¼	22½		22¾
Front length (cm)	65.5	66	66.5	67	68	68.5	69	69.5
Front length (in.)	25¾	26	26¼	26½	26¾	27	27¼	27½
Back length (cm)	59.5	60	60.5	61	62	62.5	63	63.5
Back length (in.)	23½	23¾	23¾	24	24½	24½	24¾	25

THE SEWING STARTS HERE

Assemble the bodice and facing

1 Assemble the bodice and facing, following steps 1–12 of the Sleeveless Shell Top (pages 216–217).

Insert the sleeves

2 With right sides together, matching the notches, insert the sleeves into the armholes (see page 43). Finish the seam allowances (see page 38) and press towards the sleeves.

Sew the side seams, elasticated cuffs and hem

3 Finish the raw edges of the front and back bodice side seams. With right sides together, pin and sew the underarm and side seams. Finish the seam allowances and press the seams open.

4 Around the ends of the sleeves, turn 6 mm (¼ in.) and then a further 2 cm (¾ in.) to the wrong side and press. Pin and edge stitch along the fold to create a channel for the elastic, leaving a gap of about 7 cm (3 in.).

5 Stretch elastic around your wrist and work out what's a comfortable length. Cut two pieces of elastic to this length plus 3 cm (1¼ in.). Attach a safety pin to one end of each length of elastic, then feed the elastic through the channel. Pin ends of the elastic together, then zig-zag stitch to form a loop. Edge stitch (see page 39) the gap to close it.

6 Around the hem, turn 6 mm (¼ in.) and then by a further 2 cm (¾ in.) to the wrong side. Pin in place, then stitch all around. Press the hem.

Index

Acknowledgements

LOVE PRODUCTIONS would like to thank the author Juliet Uzor for producing such a wonderful accompaniment to series 7 and 8 of *The Great British Sewing Bee*. It is so fitting that Juliet, who was our worthy winner of Series 5, would go on to author this fantastic book and pass on her expertise. We would also like to thank the talented team at Quadrille for their hard work and dedication – Sarah Lavelle, Harriet Butt, Lisa Fiske, Rebecca Smedley, Laura Eldridge and Katie Jarvis and the clever person behind the design, Emily Lapworth, who has helped to produce such a beautiful book. Our truly inspirational sewers - from Series 7; Adam, Adeena, Andrew, Cathryn, Damien, Fari, Jean, Julie, Lawratu, Raph, Rebecca and Serena and from Series 8; Angela, Annie, Brogan, Gill, Chichi, Christian, Debra, Man Yee, Marni, Mitch, Richy and Steve. We would like to thank our brilliant judges, Patrick Grant and Esme Young, for everything they have taught us about design and technique. A big thank you to our Sewing Producer Sue Suma and her sewing team, who are the backbone of the show. Our hosts Joe Lycett and Sara Pascoe, who have been so much fun across both series. For commissioning a 7th and 8th series and for all their support, we would like to thank the BBC, particularly Catherine Catton and Patrick McMahon. And finally, thank you to our viewers who give us such warm feedback on *The Great British Sewing Bee* and who like it so much that they bought this book.

JULIET UZOR As a Great British Sewing Bee alumnus, I feel very honoured to work on *The Modern Wardrobe*. Right from the very first phone call with Harriet, till this moment, I continue to have frequent 'pinch me' moments because I have been a great fan of all the books from the *Sewing Bee*.

However, writing the book would not have been possible without the support of my amazing circle. From my wonderful husband, Ken, to my beautiful daughter, Olivia – the inspiration and encouragement from them have been incredible. My extended family have also been a great support network to me over the past year, especially my sisters Chiamaka and Nwanyieze, whose weekly phone calls kept me going through difficult times and tight deadlines. I would also like to thank my wonderful girlfriends Lori, Simone and Florida, whose kind support and regular check-ins pulled me through and kept me going.

The creation of this book would not have been possible without the exceptional teamwork and support from the great team at Hardie Grant, Quadrille, including Harriet, Emily and Sarah – my amazing editor. Not forgetting the wonderful team at Grade House, especially Zuhair and Fiona. I feel very grateful to have worked with them all through the fun and tricky parts of the book creation process and the tight schedules.

There are so many people who worked very hard behind the scenes to make this book a success and I would be very ungrateful if I failed to thank my amazing online community including my Instagram and YouTube folks, not forgetting our podcast listeners and my crafty friends and podcast co-hosts Atia and Alice, who have been there for me from the start! A lot of the ideas I have considered in the book have come from comments and feedback from the community. This acknowledgement would be incomplete without a huge thank you to my fellow sewing bees: you all rock!

This book is published to accompany the television series entitled *The Great British Sewing Bee,* first broadcast on BBC TWO in 2013

Executive Producers Richard McKerrow, Sara Ramsden and Susanne Rock
Series Producer Catherine Lewendon
Series Directors Damian Eggs and Ivan Youlden
Casting Holly Flynn and Georgia Kessler
Senior Producer Keira Burgess
Sewing Producer Sue Suma
Production Executive Fin O'Riordan
Production Manager Euan McRae
Director of Legal & Commercial Affairs Rupert Frisby
Publicity Amanda Console and Shelagh Pymm
BBC Commissioning Editor Patrick McMahon
BBC Head of Popular Factual & Factual Entertainment Catherine Catton

Published in 2022 by Quadrille
an imprint of Hardie Grant Publishing

Quadrille
52–54 Southwark Street
London SE1 1UN
quadrille.com

Managing Director Sarah Lavelle
Senior Commissioning Editor Harriet Butt
Project Editor Sarah Hoggett
Assistant Editor Oreolu Grillo
Art Director & Designer Emily Lapworth
Designer Sarah Fisher
Cover Photographer Charlotte Medlicott
Photographer Brooke Harwood
Stylist Charlotte Melling
Hair & Make-up Cat Parnell, Danni Hooker and Yolanda Coetzer
Models Alejandra, Amandine, Charlie Brogan, Juliet Uzor, Kimberley Watson, Lee Ranns, Lucy Moore and Sachi
Illustrators Kate Simunek, Suzie London and Jem Venn
Pattern Grading Grade House
Makers Deborah Wilkins, Gabi Wyatt, Molly Fraser, Pippa Schulp and Susan Young
Testers Anja Burger-Kock, Beth Harley, Catheline Norte, Charlotte Powell, Emiko Kitchen, Jana Srna, Kirsty Maurits, Marine Boutroue and Tyla Thackwray
Head of Production Stephen Lang
Production Controller Katie Jarvis and Lisa Fiske

British Library Cataloguing-in-Publication Data
A catalogue record for this book is available from the British Library.

ISBN 978 1 78713 763 9

Reprinted in 2022, 2023
10 9 8 7 6 5 4 3

Printed and bound in China.

PATTERN MARKINGS & TERMINOLOGY

The pattern sheets included with the book are marked with indications such as how many of each piece you need to cut out for your project, bust darts, waist darts, grain lines and notches.

When you have cut out your fabric pieces, but before you remove the paper patterns, you will need to transfer the markings to your fabric.

General information

Each pattern piece includes the pattern number, sizes on that particular piece, what the piece is (e.g. FRONT), and simple cutting directions such as, 'CUT 2 FABRIC, CUT 1 INTERFACING'.

Grainline arrows: Usually these will have arrowheads at one or both ends. These lines are pinned parallel to the selvedge to ensure the pattern piece is correctly angled and cut out.

Angled grain line: 'Place to fold' lines have a right-angled arrowhead at either end to indicate that the pattern piece should be put on the fold of fabric.

Notches: These are short, straight lines on the cutting line extending into the seam allowance. They are used to match up seams, fronts to backs, sleeves to armholes. Cut these notches outwards from the cutting line and into the seam allowance, so that you don't cut inside of where the finished seam will be.

Lengthen or shorten lines: These are two parallel lines that indicate where the pattern can be made longer or shorter without distorting the garment shape.

Solid lines within the pattern: These indicate buttonhole positions and may also indicate the location of bust line, waist line and hip line.

Circles: These are used to mark the ends of openings such as zips, or the end of stitch lines such as gathers. They also mark placement of details such as darts, tabs, belt loops and pockets.

Cross: This symbol can mark the point of a dart, highlight the start and end of a particular feature such as a smocking line, or indicate the centre of a button.

Zigzag line: This line shows where to gather.

Darts: Are shown as V-shaped lines extending from the cutting line into the garment. To sew, match the two lines of the V, folding the fabric with right sides together, and stitch along the line from the widest point to the tip. Darts shape fabric to fit over body contours.

Parallel lines with circles and an arrow line at the bottom: These lines indicate the position of tucks and pleats. One line is the fold line, the other the placement line. The arrowhead indicates which direction to take the fold. To make pleats, fold the fabric from the fold line to the placement line, then press. Tack across the top of the pleats to hold them in place.